Praise for
DAVID MASON

"Mason is by no means a strict nature poet—one of his best-known poems is about helping his aging father go to the bathroom—but it's hard to overlook his reverence for the physical world in its infinite variety."
—Leath Tonino, *High Country News*

for SEA SALT (*2014*)

". . . a poet to listen to, and to trust."
—Kate Hendry, *The Dark Horse*

"*Sea Salt* is the real thing: one of our most authentic and accomplished poets at the top of his lyric form."
—Andrew Frisardi, *Angle*

for ARRIVALS (*2004*)

"The language and authenticity of poem after poem provide the pleasure of discovery."
—W. S. Merwin, Pulitzer Prize-winning author of *The Shadow of Sirius*

"Mason is a poet who justifies his claims. His forms breathe."
—Brian Phillips, *Poetry*

for THE COUNTRY I REMEMBER (*1996*)

"This 1,300-line family and national saga is narrative poetry at its best."
—*Publishers Weekly* starred review

"Readers, don't miss this book."
—*Minneapolis Star Tribune*

"This is a work of extraordinary warmth, vigor, imagination, and sympathy."
—Joyce Carol Oates, author of *them* and *Blonde*

ALSO BY DAVID MASON

POETRY
Sea Salt: Poems of a Decade
Ludlow: A Verse Novel
Arrivals
The Country I Remember
Land Without Grief (Chapbook)
The Buried Houses
Small Elegies (Chapbook)

FOR CHILDREN
Davey McGravy

ESSAYS
Voices, Places
Two Minds of a Western Poet
The Poetry of Life and the Life of Poetry

MEMOIR
News from the Village

DRAMATIC WORKS
The Mercy—A New Oresteia
After Life (Opera by Tom Cipullo)
The Scarlet Libretto (Opera by Lori Laitman)
Vedem (Oratorio by Lori Laitman)

EDITED
Contemporary American Poems (in China)
Western Wind: An Introduction to Poetry (with John Frederick Nims)
Twentieth-Century American Poetry (with Dana Gioia and Meg Schoerke)
Twentieth-Century American Poetics (with Dana Gioia and Meg Schoerke)
Rebel Angels: 25 Poets of the New Formalism (with Mark Jarman)

the SOUND

NEW & SELECTED POEMS BY

David Mason

Red Hen Press | *Pasadena, CA*

Book design by Selena Trager

Library of Congress Cataloging-in-Publication Data
Names: Mason, David, 1954–author.
Title: The sound: new and selected poems / by David Mason.
Description: Pasadena: Red Hen Press, 2017.
Identifiers: LCCN 2017033240 | ISBN 9781597096133 | eISBN 9781597097574
Classification: LCC PS3563.A7879 A6 2017 | DDC 811/.54—dc23
LC record available at https://lccn.loc.gov/2017033240

The National Endowment for the Arts, the Los Angeles County Arts Commission, the
Ahmanson Foundation, the Dwight Stuart Youth Fund, the Max Factor Family Foundation,
the Pasadena Tournament of Roses Foundation, the Pasadena Arts & Culture Commission
and the City of Pasadena Cultural Affairs Division, the City of Los Angeles Department of
Cultural Affairs, the Audrey & Sydney Irmas Charitable Foundation, the Kinder Morgan
Foundation, the Allergan Foundation, the Riordan Foundation, and the Amazon Literary
Partnership partially support Red Hen Press.

First Edition
Published by Red Hen Press
www.redhen.org

ACKNOWLEDGMENTS

New poems in this book first appeared in the following periodicals: *Able Muse*, the *Canberra Times* (Australia), the *Colorado Independent*, *The Dark Horse* (UK), the *Dirty Goat*, the *Hopkins Review*, the *Hudson Review*, *Measure*, the *New Criterion*, *Parnassus: Poetry in Review*, *Pequod*, *Pilgrimage Magazine*, *Poetry*, *Quadrant* (Australia), the *Robert Frost Review*, *San Diego Reader*, *Southwest Review*, the *Times Literary Supplement* (UK), *Translation*, *Valparaiso Poetry Review*, *Virginia Quarterly Review*, and the *Yale Review*.

Poems from earlier collections originally appeared in these publications: the *American Scholar*, *Boulevard*, *CrossCurrents*, *The Dark Horse* (UK), *Divide*, *Harper's Magazine*, the *Hudson Review*, *Image*, *Measure*, the *New Criterion*, the *New Yorker*, *North Dakota Quarterly*, *Ploughshares*, *Poetry*, *Prairie Schooner*, *Radio Silence*, *Sequoia*, the *Sewanee Review*, *Solo*, the *Southern Review*, the *Threepenny Review*, the *Times Literary Supplement* (UK), and the *Yale Review*.

I wish to thank the editors of the following anthologies where some of these poems appeared: *Best American Poetry 2012* (Mark Doty and David Lehman), *Best American Poetry 2018* (Dana Gioia and David Lehman), *Beyond Forgetting* (Holly J. Hughes), *A Broken Heart Still Beats* (Anne McCracken and Mary Semel), *Contemporary American Poetry* (R. S. Gwynn and April Lindner), *Introduction to Poetry* (Dana Gioia and X. J. Kennedy), *Limbs of the Pine, Peaks of the Range* (David D. Horowitz), *Many Trails to the Summit* (David D. Horowitz), *Measure for Measure* (Annie Finch and Alexandra Oliver), *New Poets of the American West* (Lowell Jaeger), *The Penguin Book of Twentieth-Century American Poetry* (Rita Dove), *Poetry Out Loud* (Dan Stone and Stephen Young), *Poetry: A Pocket Anthology* (R. S. Gwynn), *Poets Translate Poets* (Paula Deitz), *Rhyming Poems* (William Baer), *Story Hour* (Sonny Williams), and *The Wadsworth Anthology of Poetry* (Jay Parini).

Thanks as well to these websites where some poems appeared: Academy of American Poets (Poem-a-Day), American Life in Poetry, Poetry Daily, and The Writer's Almanac.

Aralia Press, Dacotah Territory Press, JonesAlley Press, and The Press at Colorado College published chapbooks and limited editions in which some of these poems appeared. I wish to thank in particular Aaron Cohick, Brian Molanphy, Michael Peich, Sally Quinn, Joan Stone, and Mark Vinz for their fine work.

Poetry publishers do heroic labor for little reward. I owe a particular debt to Mark Cull, Kate Gale, and Robert McDowell, all three of whom have put their lives on the line for poetry.

for Chrissy

CONTENTS

From *Sea Salt: Poems of a Decade* (2014)

From *Arrivals* (2004)

From *The Country I Remember* (1996)

From *Land Without Grief* (1996)

From *The Buried Houses* (1991)

THE SOUND

WALKING BACKWARDS
An Author's Note

The Sound is a location, my place of origin and womb of words, but it is also an aspiration and aural guide. "The sound is the gold in the ore," Frost wrote. One hears something and wants to make a corresponding sound. I have been hard of hearing all my life, catching vowels more than consonants, so the sound I follow is watery. I hope you can hear it too.

Assembling this book has allowed me to revise some earlier work. No revision in a poem is minor, but some changes may be noticeable only to me. I have not grouped poems by subject or genre, but have allowed for accidental discoveries as well as a kind of walking backwards.

A writer of narrative and dramatic poetry requires more room than a writer of lyrics. Excerpting long poems is unfair to them, but one also wants to represent the range of effort over decades. Here readers will find the maverick products of a writer who does not want to repeat himself. I have not excerpted my verse novels, plays, and libretti but have made room to put one longer poem, "The Country I Remember," back into print.

I am not the product of a creative writing program but of my own dilatory learning. Yet I have been lucky in my friendships with other writers, several of whom have offered advice and assistance over the years. They know who they are. My greatest debt is acknowledged in the book's dedication.

NEW POEMS

Descend

And what of those who have no voice
and no belief, dumbstruck and hurt by love,
no bathysphere to hold them in the depths?
Descend with them and learn and be reborn
to the changing light. We all began without it,
and some were loved and some forgot the love.
Some withered into hate and made a living
hating and rehearsing hate until they died.
The shriveled ones, chatter of the powerful—
they all go on. They go on. You must descend
among the voiceless where you have a voice,
barely a whisper, unheard by most, a wave
among the numberless waves, a weed torn
from the sandy bottom. Here you are. Begin.

THE WORLD OF HURT

Where are its borders—the world of hurt?
Not in these woods outside the window,
not in the helpful drone of the sea.

But the mind has trouble neglecting the news,
the acid comment, expedient bombing
and frontiers brimming with refugees.

She turned from the pictures to face me, the hurt
taking hold in her eyes. Right then I saw
from the ragged green of the woods, the bird

that had come for itself in the window, and banked
before impact, and left like a song
and was gone to die some other way.

A skill of intelligent flight. Or luck.
Her look changed when I told her about it.
The bird that flew off into the world.

Woman Dressing by a Window

There's a fire between touch
and touch like the heat of noon
between moon and moon
moving a soul to such

a silent howl,
an exultation of skin.
O how could one begin
when words can only crawl

where they would leap
in every glance
like a fountain's dance
before a long and tidal sleep?

Now she turns
to her own tasks
and nothing in her asks
that one should burn

or learn by letting be—
like time, like day and night,
like any new delight
set free.

THE SOUND

It wasn't the drunken skipper in the dream
commanding me to *Listen up* or find
my head in the bay. It wasn't the net drum,

the power block for brailing the wet line
or classes of salmon I was so inclined
to school with, breathing in the kelp and brine.

It wasn't the purling motor of the skiff
dragging the weighty net to its fleeting purse
but the sea itself, the Sound and my belief

instructing me this work was nothing worse
than setting out and hauling in a seine,
and setting out and hauling it in again,

getting used to the play of hand and mind.
Listen up, he said, *and set a course.*
I said I work alone like all my kind.

Ah, self-employed. He went below to doze
in the iced hold. *You would be one of those.*

I headed for the point beyond the point
and stripped and greased myself with oolichan
and swam the echoes to oblivion.

COMBINE

The tractor puffing diesel
crawled along the swath,
the hayfork pulling vines
into the combine's maw,
and the high bin filled
with damp green peas—
a boy's first shirtless job,
baked nut-brown from dark
all through the burning day
until the Sound beyond
the dikes bled red.
Gulls in the fields, crows
in the bramble hedges,
a field mouse squirming
on the fork boy's tines
and the old mechanic standing
in white overalls mid-field
as if he'd lost his train
of thought.
       Those hands of his,
work-swollen knuckles,
grease in the whorls a boy
discerned his future in,
even the one finger nipped off
at the top joint, even that
old pain recovered from
was prophecy of a kind
(we all bleed and lose
the fortune-teller says).

The work was slow enough
for thought, still more for books
read in all weathers
when the bosses left,
and reading under the sky
to the smell of marsh salt
and chaff and rotting vines,
education's skin and bone
for learning's ache
and the ache of learning,
gone to school in work
and for a time a living
wage to wage a life.

THE GIFTS OF TIME

To stand in the kitchen high up in the trees
watching a sapling sway, the canopy
of leaves and needles stirred by an undersea,
and stare, a mug of coffee in the hand,
is all of time. No necessary task
impels a rush to dress and find the keys.
Decades have served for that. It's time to breathe.

Time also for a long gray ship to turn
and for a young man standing on the bridge
to wonder if that distant speck is bird
or continent. The young man, older now,
can hear the heartbeat of an ailing girl.
He moves the stethoscope, tells her to breathe,
and knows the murmur is her leaking blood,

and he is only one, and in the time
it takes to breathe he too is gone forever.
He too is like the stir of swaying trees,
the muddy cliffs eroded by the surf.
Stand here and listen to the trees and know
their generation too will fall away.
The cliffs will fall away. The voices die.

There was another ship, another time,
but going nowhere. It steamed both day and night.
It made quite a business of making clouds.
The sky poured from its stack, its boilers the same,
and the ship's hull tugged at cables and lines

lashed to a gravel bulkhead by the road.
It tugged like a leashed dog with boundless hope
but never left the shore, that cloudy ship
with laborers who strove inside the hull.

It rained inside. The men were always wet,
the women too, working wet, and wet
when they quit work and stepped out to the clouds
exhaled from cigarettes they cupped in hands,
talking of food they would like to eat again
and letters they would like to read, dry-eyed.
They too felt time rising from the gray stack.
Time is the kitchen high up in the trees
and time is the cloudy ship, time is the shore.

The people hadn't known the time before.
Only when it slowed and swayed and clouded out,
only when the coffee in the hand went cool
could anyone be sure they'd touched the hours
or the year of gull cries from an open throat.
A current stirs the trees like tidal grass.
Stand in the kitchen looking out to sea
through stands of waving limbs and feel the wind,
the leaking vessels of the blood go down.

No one can make up time. The sea would laugh,
the crowded rocks whisper among themselves.
The coffee has gone cold. The names are gone.
They are another generation gone.

The room is time, the room is out of time.
The fissured road will fall into the waves.
The ruined millionaire will watch his house
tip like a sandbox toy and slide away.

A colony of ants will have its say
remembered by the beetle rolling dung.
An old man dances, knowing he is young.
A woman dances in the breaking day.

GALLINA CANYON

All night the cattle bellowed,
cows and calves of the separated herd
seeking each other under helpless stars,
never sleeping, even when the dog slept.

Cows and calves of the separated herd,
loud as the far-flung buffalo
never sleeping, even when the dog slept.
I heard a world of other animals,

loud as the far-flung buffalo,
loud as mother bears calling to their young.
I heard a world of other animals
filling the canyon with their awful song.

Loud as mother bears calling to their young,
a night of wailing from the walls,
filling the canyon with their awful song
from open lungs among the cottonwoods.

A night of wailing from the walls.
I could not sleep. The night was at a loss.
From open lungs among the cottonwoods,
mothers were calling to their young.

I could not sleep. The night was at a loss.
All night the cattle bellowed.
Mothers were calling to their young,
seeking each other under helpless stars.

SAYING GRACE

If every moment is
and is a wilderness
to navigate by feel
whether half or whole,
the river takes a turn,
the forest has to burn,
the broken fern to grow.

The silence of a night
of supplicating stars
may answer us aright:
our worries and our cares
are not the same as theirs.
Give us this day more world
than we can ever know.

BRISTLECONE PINE

If wind were wood it might resemble this
fragility and strength, old bark bleeding amber.
Its living parts grow on away from the dead
as we do in our lesser lives. Endurance,
yes, but also a scarred and twisted beauty
we know the way we know our own carved hearts.

To the Sea of Cortez

for Robert King

And if I could I would
fall down, fall all the way
down to the breathing sea.
I would pass by the towns
I would pass by the grass
banks where the buffalo graze.
I would fall down, I would
lie down in the red mud
of memory, where Spanish
lances lie with arrowheads.
I would lie down and roll
my being to the sea,
unroll and roll, lap and sing
my body down, and down
and turn at the hard cliffs
and carry the soft soil
with me. Nothing would impede
my downward being, my
desire to lie down like a fawn
in the new grass, like trout
in the shallows, like a child
tired of making letters
out of chalk, or talk
of airy nothings caught
by fingers made of lead.
I would lie down and go,
and go until I found
the sea that rose to meet
whatever thread of me
had made it there, out there
among vaquitas and swift birds,

there where hardy grasses
have not been annihilated,
where the salt tides rise,
looking for currents they
have loved, and finding me.

THE SECRET HEARING

A life that moves to music cannot fail . . .
—A. D. Hope

Big as a pterodactyl and as old
it seemed. *Damn.* The muscled force of air.
The straight flight
heedless of gardeners. That was the wild.

No one stood near to see the heron beat
above my head, making me dive for cover
in the autumn flowerbed.
No one saw me kneeling to watch it pass.

Even the marriage I went home to later,
a solitude of children who wouldn't tell,
knew banishment
unspoken, and fiercely tribal distances.

But I had felt the air pushed from its wings.
I raked and hauled the cartloads of dead leaves
behind my tractor,
singing a made-up tune no person heard,

half-worshipping the world that made such flight,
feeling its hidden music in my lungs,
but safe in the sound
of the diesel engine drowning out my voice.

MENDING TIME

The fence was down. Out among humid smells
and shrill cicadas we walked, the lichened trunks
moon-blue, our faces blue and our hands.

Led by their bellwether bellies, the sheep
had toddled astray. The neighbor farmer's woods
or coyotes might have got them, or the far road.

I remember the night, the moon-colored grass
we waded through to look for them, the oaks
tangled and dark, like starting a story midway.

We gazed over seed heads to the barn
toppled in the homestead orchard. Then we saw
the weather of white wool, a cloud in the blue

moving without sound as if charmed
by the moon beholding them out of bounds.
Time has not tightened the wire or righted the barn.

The unpruned orchard rots in its meadow
and the story unravels, the sunlight creeping back
like a song with nobody left to hear it.

Across the Pyrenees

We had to change—Iberian rails
were a wider gauge. The tricorn hats
of the *Guardia Civil* glared in the rain.
Their submachine guns glared, and that's

how we knew Franco was still alive.
The sleepy passengers packed in,
leaned on baskets or thigh to thigh
as steel on steel made a lurching whine

and we were moving through the night,
the Spanish night, the civil war
of books fresh in my memory
and in the looks these faces bore,

till a man whose thin, unshaven face
was wan with sleeplessness pulled down
a *bota* full of wine and squeezed
a long stream into his open mouth

and smiled, passing the bag to me.
I grasped the full goatskin of wine.
He showed me how to tip my head
and squeeze the skin until a line

of fruit and sunlight filled my mouth
with a sweat and leather aftertaste.
I passed the skin to a young girl
across from me who wore a chaste

black sweater, but drank the wine
in a long, slow, practiced pull
and shook her pretty head and laughed.
The old man called it "blood of the bull,"

slicing slabs of cheese with a knife
while his plump wife busied herself
paring apples from a plastic sack
she'd taken down from the luggage shelf.

These too were passed among us, bread
and wine, cheese and fruit, and I
had nothing to offer my companions
but a word of thanks they waved away.

Yes—it happened many years ago
in the passing dark of northern Spain.
Some strangers shared their food with me
in the dim light of the night train.

Sketches in the Sun

Folksong (Anonymous)

I kissed red lips and my lips too were dyed,
and the handkerchief I wiped them with turned red,
and the running stream where I washed that kerchief
colored the shoreline far out into mid-sea.
An eagle swooped down for a drink, and its wings
as it rose stained half the sun, all of the moon.

The Laurel (Achilles Paraschos)

Don't envy me. Don't envy the laurel tree,
    my roots watered with blood and scalding tears.
Only those who never look for me
    are lucky, who seek the rose in their careers.
The sick and disinherited I crown
    singly, weaving my envy-poisoned leaves,
a life of pain refining their renown.
    Only the poets truly win my wreaths.

❖❖❖

The Cypress Tree (Kostis Palamas)

I look out the window; the depth
    of sky, all sky and nothing more;
    and within it, utterly sky-swept,
    a slender cypress; nothing more.

Whether sky is starry or dark,
   in drunken blue or thunder's roar,
   always the cypress sways, so stark,
   calm, lovely, hopeless; nothing more.

The Ship (C. P. Cavafy)

It certainly resembles him,
this small penciled portrait.

Hurriedly drawn on the ship's deck
one delightful afternoon.
The Ionian Sea surrounding us.

It resembles him. Yet I remember a greater beauty.
He was painfully sensitive
and this lit up his expression.
He seems to me more beautiful
now when my soul recalls him from the years.

From the years. All of those things are very old—
the sketch, the ship and the afternoon.

Lean Girls (Yannis Ritsos)

Lean girls are gathering salt by the shore,
bending to bitterness, ignorant of the open sea.

A sail, a white sail, beckons from the blue,
and what they do not see in the distance
    darkens with longing.

September 1971 (Yiorgos Chouliaras)

Summer incessantly flees from open windows
light burns
the room is flooded with butterflies

at such a time he too
was looking for the dead king's face
in a gold reflection

the boat was rocking
in the mind's furrows
and the field split in two
where the armored sun's bright thorns
rose up

the place smelled of basil
maybe this is the message
of the one we are looking for
in the stone, the birds and the ship

Many names from those days
remain unchanged
but we, what do we know
Ασίνην τε—
a word in Seferis

FIRST CHRISTMAS IN THE VILLAGE

It was unanticipated, the birth,
and late at that, stormy and close,
as we were gathered in by the hearth.
Nothing about it called for words,
though the widow had no children
and taught a game with playing cards.

A fisherman brought an octopus
that sizzled on a metal grate
over the pulsing olive coals.
The widow's father leaned to the fire
and with a dark blade sawed off a leg
and laid it burning on my plate.

It tasted like a briny steak
with tentacles like tiny lips
oozing the savor of the sea,
my first octopus, its brain afire.
And the illicit cards—*Don't tell the priest*—
a wink at caution in the game of living.

That night all human struggle ended,
or recollection wants it so.
That night all murders were forgotten
in the salt abundance and the storm
and the warm fire in the widow's house
when the vast peace was said to be born.

That night I carried a bucket of coals
back to my rented dwelling, wind
trailing the fading sparks behind—
a small fire, for the warmth it made
as the stars held steady in the dome,
and sleep became an open grave.

GIVEN RAIN

Late in these latitudes,
the given rain, hazel and
evergreen by the small roads
where few are traveling,

inwards, indoors, the books
lie open, read not at random
but by dreaming whimsy
like roads in the dusk.

The child who struggled
to write a name and struggled
harder to believe that name
now moves the pen

of the one who has come indoors
and shaken the rain
and left muddy boots on the mat.
The world is wet

and close and the light
is low, the books
glow with a darkness of their own,
the words like rain in the mind.

It is late in these latitudes.
Sleep on, says the hill
of the night and the tunneling road
bent out of sight.

The Nightmare Version

You arrive at a seaside town
and the wind is blowing a gale,
soaking your clothes with rain.

By the quay you cannot fail
to notice a drowned pig
in the sea wrack and gravel,

a man shooing his dog
away from the pale flesh,
and you feel your spirits sag.

The gale-blown rollers crash
on the black piles of the pier
and it seems that every sash

and door you can see from here
is shut against your face.
Only a pint of bitter

in a dim pub solaces
as you steam in the damp air.
The barman dips his glasses,

tells you it isn't fair
and you wonder what he means.
You've come to find a lair

in the kirkyard by the fence,
a grave without a stone,
but the barman's acting dense

and leaves you there alone
to nurse the dregs of your pint.
You know you know this town,

the pier on the pummeled point,
because you've been here before—
a face in the mirror's glint,

the beer stains on the floor,
bad weather in your blood,
a pig dead on the shore.

DAYTIME

An empty room, the television on,
rooms where the baby's fed and the vacuum's run,
then elevators playing CNN,

a silent baseball game above a bar,
amoebic pictures from a distant star,
three models waving hands across a car—

I see these screens and, feeling pixelated,
dust in a sunbeam, so disintegrated
I can't divine the cases being stated,

wonder if a particle, afloat,
can teach itself to pray, or to devote
its substance to the god of the remote.

To Hygeia

Goddess, I have watched your motions gratify the world.
Votaries of all casts and ages, genders, voices,
bow to you as they must, for nothing follows without you.

I once met a man in an iron lung, puffing his words,
and youth was a much-too-long parade of unfortunate data:
the infirm, the wizened, the washout, the accidental suicide . . .

An old man with a tinkling highball sat like a lord
orating, *When I was a boy*, and we knew a story was coming.
I never minded those times, being an odd duck
who actually listened, but the lesson I failed to get was the one
he always meant: *One of these days, you smug twit,*
you'll be me.

Now my sage joints prophesy like rats
from a leaking ship, and every morning's gulp of pills
pules in silent offering to Hygeia. *Keep moving*
until you stop. The hell with the good opinion of others.
Wisdom of age, goddess—the sort we laugh about
if lucky enough.

In dreams I'm still the boy who listens.
Others suffer sleepless nights, others find the day
too hard to climb, but climb to summits anyway.
Think of them, betrayed by their own bones or blood,
bent inside with maladies no one else can see,
for whom merely to walk a city block would be
a woozy flight.

So I've become a spinner of yarns—
hopefully not a sower of yawns—my hearing aids,
crow's feet and specs, and all my hidden pangs and pains
pleading the Fifth before I find a fifth and pour
a neat inch at cocktail time. *Look with thine ears,*
said Lear to the world prolonging. Well, I've been there,
half-hearing my way through human mazes.

                                    When I was a boy
I listened to men weathered and withered, withstanding all
the way they'd ducked at mortar fire or kamikazes,
and women who took my arm to make it to the car.
I chauffeured the old, cajoled them to keep up the work of living,
helped them to their doors, found keys, conveyed them
to dough-smelling kitchens, pans of foiled leftovers,
letters they'd never written, love they'd never conveyed,
whatever decay of night was left to wander in.

Now I've only to hallow their too-neglected names
with yours, goddess, each time I offer a lit candle
or swallow the pills and pride or raise my ringing glass.

The New Dope

It was softer on the throat,
harder on the heart.

Two tokes deep in the lungs
and I saw double,

troubled my friends, I didn't feel
so well, so well.

It was a kind of hell
of harmlessness, except

the sad division of the world
I feared was permanent,

no longer sane or self,
no longer sole or whole

so long as brick streets multiplied
on the long, the short, the long drive home.

So long, I said. It took so long
to say *So long*.

Next day I was glad
that gravity was back, and this

abyss-less ordinary mug
of coffee in my hands.

DISTURBED PARADELLE

Do not repeat yourself.
Do not repeat yourself.
Habits are hard to break.
Habits are hard to break.
Repeat: Hard. Break. Habits
Are not to do yourself.

Why do you look that way?
Why do you look that way?
Am I so very strange to you?
Am I so very strange to you?
To look way strange, why that?
So you do. I am very you.

The days go slipping by.
The days go slipping by
Before you can catch them.
Before you can catch them.
Slipping before you go,
Catch them. Days. By the can.

Habits catch you slipping
By yourself. Look to the
Hard days. Am I to go?
Way before them, do not
Break. You repeat why so you are
That can do. Very strange.

THE GREAT CHANGER

Without a song to find a lover by,
some days she floated like a driftwood log,
beached at high tide beneath a dismal sky.
She was not Salmon Woman swimming under fog.

She was not Echo, nor was she Talking River.
She was not Thunder and she was not ever
the mouse who changed her skin for woman's skin.
She was not Milky Way. She was not Moon.

She had to move a mountain with a spoon
and never ask forgiveness of the sun.
When change came it was a gradual dying.
She was not Owl Woman. This was not flying.

But she was Fox and found her gnawed-off limb
and the Great Changer came. And she welcomed him.

Horse People

When Quanah Parker's mother as a young girl
saw her family lanced and hacked to pieces,
and was herself thrown on the hurtling rump
of a warrior's pony whipped to the far off
and utterly unwritten Comancheria,
the little blonde began her life, outcast
only when the whites recaptured her and killed
the man she loved, the father of her children.

The language she forgot would call her ruined
and beyond redemption like the young she suckled,
among them the "last Chief of the Comanche,"
a man who died in comforts his mother spurned,
but who, like her, remembered how the manes
of the remuda caught the breezes as they ran,
and how the grass caught fire in the scalp-red sun.

SAND CREEK

The land flayed open like a skin
on which the stories would be drawn

The sky a turtled bowl, powdered
blue of a broken robin's egg

and there beside the washboard road
where the wire fences lean and sing

rust-colored feathers of a hawk
a turret-turning beak and eye

I bend a knee
and lean on shatterings of rock

to watch a beetle right itself
and struggle into stems and weeds

a cricket like an autumn leaf
crackling in crooked flight

The compass draws around me blue
A whittled bone-white moon fades west

and there is unheard lamentation here
and there is blood, blood everywhere

the dried blood color of the weeds
the blood of recollection, true

or not true as the case may be
The hawk, the beetle and the rest

go on, the stream goes on, the trees
all offering, all lifted high

and opened like the land, the skin
with its evaporating stain.

FRANGIPANI

Cut blossoms floating in a bowl of water
are what they are. Someone saw and gathered
the pale white and yellow stars and leaned

intimately down. To know the fragile blooms
with breathing color is to be reborn
astir, astray, and happier than before.

They float to survive now, a mystery like the dead
wake up to in the cradle of the night,
flesh of frangipani sweetening the bed

between the mown grass and the Southern Cross,
and if the memory bleeds at such a loss
it's only the cost of living with desire.

So let the sphinx moths hunting nectar there
where none exists be go-betweens for life,
purposefully duped. Let the perfume rise.

GALAHS IN THE WIND

The tents are coming loose,
whole households on a string
and no one knows just where
the children have run off to.

Oh joy, the limbs and leaves
are tearing like the waves.
We are galahs. Galahs in the wind!
The sunlight shouts and we

tsup-tsup in riotous flight.
The world is all a seed to eat,
a song to answer everywhere,
we must be everywhere

at once we must, we must
tsup-tsup to the sun
our flight beneath the blue
and endless racing heaven.

MY SCOTTISH GRANDMOTHER'S LOBOTOMY

The tool used hardly mattered.
The procedure could be done
even with a screwdriver
slipped in through the eye socket,
scraping pre-frontal tissue,
and what was lost—neurosis
or addiction, flights of high
or crashing spirits—mattered
to a world made calmer. *Thus.*

And thus it was, the patient
lost the village window she
had once crawled out of, fleeing
her carpenter father's house,
lost the need to find escape,
pilfered morphine, syringes
slipped from hospital closets,
lost years of nurse's training,
lost her own words—you might say

lost her mind, the part of her
those who loved her thought they loved,
got rid of now. The mad girl
wrecked and pinioned in a bed,
aired in a hospital chair,
out of it, mouthing drivel.
She lived that way for decades.
I never heard her accent,
her laughter, even a cough.

Bildungsroman

i. m. Seamus Heaney

Because for us all things were living
the night train could not pass unwatched—
the way it threw the forest shadows
spinning across our bedroom wall,
the way it shook the house, the way
the revving diesel blew its top—
so I climbed the metal ladder up
to the upper bunk to see the light
that cast the passing images,
and somehow slipped and stuck my foot
right through the bedroom window glass.
No cut but a shock of the real
and a brother's mockery for trying
to see beyond, and a moment's crying.

HANGMAN

A Big Chief tablet and a Bic
between us on the car's back seat,
the scaffold drawn, and underneath
a code of dashes in a row
for seven letters. Part of a stick-
figure fixed to the noose's O

for every letter missed, until
if I'm not careful my poor guy
will hang with x's for his eyes.
My brother parlays his resource
for big boy words with taunting skill:
"It starts with *d* and rhymes with *force.*"

But I don't know the word, don't know
the wet world being slapped away
by wiper blades, or why the day
moved like an old stop-action film
or an interrupted TV show
about a family on the lam.

I let myself be hanged, and learn
a new word whispered out of fear,
though it will be another year
before I feel the house cut loose,
my dangling body and the burn
of shame enclosing like a noose.

SECURITY LIGHT

The glow outside our window is no fallen star.
It is futility itself. It is the fear of night
a neighbor burns with, nightmare of a stubborn child.

I dreamed of chasing crows in a dark of sea fog
and no wind, the chill smell of kelp and changing things,
knowing the sea's edge and the sand met where the fish lived.

I saw the waters running out to meet the water
coming in, the small crabs lifted off their claws.
I saw the trysting place of cormorants, the cliffs

of guarded nests where eagles watched like sated kings
alive, alive at the moving sand clock of the sea
where all's dissolved, where earth itself is taken down.

THE STUDENT

Just hours before he went to hang himself
he smiled at me and promised poems would come,
then waved goodbye, apprentice to the word.

He lived. But in fractions. A feeding tube
uncoiling from his abdomen. His aunt
and mother held him still to shave his face.

I bent and kissed the boy. He mouthed the air
and murmured what we hoped was meaning speech.
He wasn't fully made when he strung up

his life. His instrument was still untuned.
That was a year ago. Word comes of struggle,
as if a strangled soul would find the strength

to love what wasn't wholly there before,
only the promised happiness of song
beyond the comprehension of the mind.

What else could explain the effort to crawl back
among the living, for whom speech is easy
but understanding never comes in peace?

Old Man Walking

The old man walking on the road
alone, with stark trees and a sky
as gray-white as his heavy head,
had lifted many a thought on high,

had lifted them to dream-head trees,
the witnesses of all the weight
dropping the old man to his knees
when no one saw him in the night.

Days when he did not dare to write,
the black dog for his only friend,
he stepped out on the road, the white
unwritten sky without an end.

An old man never walks alone.
Let others judge what others see.
The old man walking on the road
had words to keep him company.

PASSION

It isn't the choir of small boys, casting about, singing shyly or
    with perfect oval mouths,
and it isn't the gentle rocking solo on the violin
played by a man who'd sooner mooch a meal from anyone than
    pay,
and it isn't the lovely rapture of the cellist who, between her legs
    and in the fluent embrace of her arms,
gives birth to a god who makes the audience tremble,
and it isn't the white-haired athlete marking time with his stick
    and coaxing the lot of them to music,
and it isn't the long-dead Lutheran *Kapellmeister* who built this
    temple of sound with a crew of amateurs,
and it isn't the packed house too eager to spring to its feet in
    applause,
or the flaws of performance, or the whole tragic lift of the night
    as the story surges to its close.
It is all of them. And it passes. And will never be heard again
    on earth.

THE SHOW

At first you can almost believe
by the breeze in the outdoor café's slender trees
and the family outing atmosphere
among the approving people gathered here
the night will turn to poetry,
but the angry man at the microphone
appears to think that he and he alone
by virtue of his earnest shout
can turn opinions into art.
One longs for a quiet thought
no one applauds,
and words that are not clods.

Michael Donaghy 1954–2004

Like a wash of paint on board, transparent figures,
unsolid as shadows and the passing river . . .
I look at them, and look again, again—
a lifetime passing in a shower of rain.

We Stand Together Talking

We stand together talking, like making love
in a burning city where forsaken love

hurls stones and bullets, and the livid face
declares it never had a stake in love.

Where love requires denying other love
like hammers driving nails in, breaking love.

From sleep I find you rising from your sleep
and kiss your eyes, so full of aching love.

My love, the harm was hidden, but the hate
would damn us living for the sake of love.

EPIGRAM

The baby's bawling and the old man's laughter
rise from the center of the same *I am.*
Say it to windows, doors. Say it to rafters
on rivers of light. Say it to the breaking dam.

from SEA SALT: POEMS OF A DECADE

2014

KÉFI

Every meal a communion.
The uninvited dead are here.
Do they miss the taste of wine
or the flickering glare

of the candle in the window?
I remember some of their names.
Their appetites are hollow.
They crowd like moths to the flame

but the poor things cannot burn.
Light-headed in this company,
I look at them all in turn.
The Greeks would call this *kéfi*,

ineffable, weightless, tuned
to the conversations of the night
with or without a moon.
O everything's all right.

It's *kéfi*—coffee would wreck it,
or too much wine, but a song
if I can remember it
will carry us along.

NEW WORLD

Snow in the pines, spring snow, and a white cloud
glowering, smoke blown from that old pacer
who pauses for all day, and then moves on.

The felled trees lie in the steaming forest
lit by the far coals of the world's beginning.
The fox darts over jeweled kinnikinnik—

Be quick, be quick, say the black beads of his eyes,
and with any luck our eyes will follow him
as far as a look can take us, darting through sleep

to a new thought, another chance at waking.

A Thorn in the Paw

Once I was a young dog with a big thorn
in its paw, slowly becoming that very thorn,
not the howl but the thing
howled at, importunate, printing in blood.

Others grew up with chrism, incense, law,
but I was exiled from the start to stare
at lightning hurled from the sky
into a lake that revealed only itself.

Others had pews and prayer-shawls, old fathers
telling them when to kneel and what to say.
I had only my eyes
my tongue my nose my skin and feeble ears.

Dove of descent, fat worm of contention,
bogeyman, Author—I can't get rid of you
merely by hating the world
when people behave at their too-human worst.

Birds high up in their summer baldachin
obey the messages of wind and leaves.
Their airy hosannas
can build a whole day out of worming and song.

I've worked at the thorn, I've stood by the shore
of the marvelous, drop-jawed and jabbering.
Nobody gave me a god
so I perfect my idolatry of doubt.

THE TELLER

He told me, maybe thirty years ago,
he'd met a rawboned Eskimo named Jack
while filming polar bears on an ice floe.
Jack went out fishing in his sealskin kayak
but the current carried him so far off course
that when a Russian freighter rescued him
they signed him as a mate to Singapore.
Five years at sea it took to get back home.

The year an Englishman gave him his name.
The year of hustling on a Bali beach.
The year of opium in Vietnam.
The year he pined for snow. The year he searched
for any vessel that would turn toward Nome.
The man who told me? I tell you, I don't know.

THE FAWN

❖

The vigil and the vigilance of love . . .

Sitter to three towheaded, rowdy boys,
the spoiled offspring of the local doctor,
our cousin Maren came north for a summer
and brought us stories of the arid south—
cowpokes and stone survivals.

               One afternoon
she summoned two of us to the garage,
a leaning shed with workbench, vise, and tools
stood up between dark studs and logging chains.
A cobwebbed window faced the windy lake
and let in light that squared off on the floor,
and there, quick-breathing on the cracked concrete,
a wounded fawn's black eyes looked back at us.
Maren told how a neighbor's dog had caught it,
showed us the wheezing holes made by the teeth,
the spotted fur blood-flecked, the shitty haunch
where it had soiled itself in the lunged attack.
Don't know where its mama got to, Maren said.
Poor thing's scared. Don't touch it. Run get a bowl
for water.

            When I came back she made a bed
of tarps and grass. Our tomboy cousin had hauled
that wounded fawn down from the neighbor's field.
Now she nursed it until dusk. Our father
stopped by with his satchel after rounds

and Maren held the fawn so he could listen.
Shaking his head, he sat back on his heels,
removed the stethoscope. He called the vet
who told him there was nothing they could do
but wait it out.

        I don't know, our father said.
Sometimes you shouldn't interfere with nature.

A mean dog isn't nature, Maren said.

Well I'm not blaming you for being kind.

Our father brought a blanket from the house,
a baby bottle filled with milk, and he
and Maren shared the vigil for the fawn,
leaving a light on as they might for a child
sick in some farmer's house.

        Three days—a week—
and father backed the car to the garage
to carry out the dead fawn in a tarp
and bury it in some deep part of the woods,
unmarked, and later unremarked upon
with summer over and our cousin gone.

If I tell you it was 1963
you'll know a world of change befell us next,

but maybe it was '62. I know
it was before the war divided us
and more than that, before our parents grew
apart like two completely different species,
desert and woods, cactus and thorny vine,
before our nation had its family quarrel,
never quite emerging from it. We boys
had sprouted into trouble of all kinds,
three would-be rebels from a broken home,
and when I next saw Maren, a rancher's wife
in Colorado, she was all for Jesus,
getting saved and saving every day
in some denomination she invented.
We gave up calling and we never write.

The vigil and the vigilance. Our troubles
happened, but were smaller than a country's.
My older brother died at twenty-eight—
an accident in mountains. Our mother sobered
up two decades later. Father died
so far removed from his former sanity
I struggle to remember who he was.

The years are a great winnowing of lives,
but we had knelt together by the fawn
and felt the silence intervene like weather.
I'm still there, looking at that dying fawn,
at how a girl's devotion almost saved it,
wet panic in its eyes, its shivering breath,
its wild heart beating on the concrete floor.

FATHERS AND SONS

Some things, they say,
one should not write about. I tried
to help my father comprehend
the toilet, how one needs
to undo one's belt, to slide
one's trousers down and sit,
but he stubbornly stood
and would not bend his knees.
I tried again
to bend him toward the seat,

and then I laughed
at the absurdity. Fathers and sons.
How he had wiped my bottom
half a century ago, and how
I would repay the favor
if he would only sit.

                    Don't you—
he gripped me, trembling, searching for my eyes.
Don't you—but the word
was lost to him. Somewhere
a man of dignity would not be laughed at.
He could not see
it was the crazy dance
that made me laugh,
trying to make him sit
when he wanted to stand.

HOME CARE

My father says his feet will soon be trees
and he is right, though not in any way
I want to know. A regal woman sees
me in the hallway and has much to say,
as if we were lovers once and I've come back
to offer her a rose. But I am here
to find the old man's shoes, his little sack
of laundered shirts, stretch pants and underwear.

Rattling a metal walker for emphasis,
his pal called Joe has one coherent line—
How the hell they get this power over us?—
then logic shatters and a silent whine
crosses his face. My father's spotted hands
flutter like dying moths. I take them up
and lead him in a paranoiac dance
toward the parking lot and our escape.

He is my boy, regressed at eighty-two
to mooncalf prominence, drugged and adrift.
And I can only play, remembering who
he was not long ago, a son bereft.
Strapped in the car, he sleeps away the hour
we're caught in currents of the interstate.
He will be ashes in a summer shower
and sink to roots beneath the winter's weight.

Mrs. Vitt

The first to realize what a liar I was,
a boy pretending to have read a book
in second grade about a big black cat
(I'd made it as far as the cover silhouette),
the first to let us choose our spelling words
like *telephone* and *information*, long
pronounceable portions of the sky outside,
words I ever after spelled correctly,
the first to tell me I was a funny boy
or had a funny sense of the truth, or had
no sense of it but was funny anyway,
Mrs. Vitt began to shake one day,
lighting her cigarette in the teachers' lounge,
or carrying coffee in her quaking hands.
I was in high school then, but heard she'd quit
and went to visit her in the old north end
of town, and met her thin, attentive husband
strapping her to a board to hold her straight.
She smiled at me, though her head shook to and fro.
It took her husband many lighter flicks
to catch her swaying cigarette. She looked
like a knife-thrower's trembling model. *Mrs. Vitt,*
I blurted out. *I'm sorry.* She stared at me,
but whether she was nodding or shaking *no*
I couldn't tell. *Sorry I lied so much.*
I must have given you a lot of grief.
And she, with each word shuddered out in smoke:
No child I taught was any grief to me.

DRIVING WITH MARLI

Grandpa, do you live in the sky?
No, but I live on a mountain
and came on a plane to see you.
Why?
All leaping thought and ruminant pool,
a three-year-old is a verbal fountain,
water clear enough to see through.
Anything can fool
the wizard in the front seat of the car.
How far will we go, Grandpa? How far?

Little one, I must relearn
all subjects such as distances,
study the foolishness and burn
like candlelight to worry less and less
about the night.
It's not that youth is always right
but that an aging man
is too preoccupied with plans.
I do live in the sky,
but I do not know why.

THE NAPE

In the cidery light of morning
I saw her at the table
reading the paper, her cup
of coffee near at hand,
and that was when I bent
and brushed the hair from her nape
and kissed the skin there, breathing
the still-surprising smoothness
of her skin against my lips—
stolen, she might say,
as if I would be filled
with joy of touching her,
I the fool for love,
and all that history carried
back to me in the glide
of mouth on skin, knowledge
of who she is by day
and night, sleeping lightly,
rocked in gentle privacy,
or outside in the garden
probing earth and planting.
We had been this way for more
than twenty years, she
leading a life of purpose
rarely stated, and I
just back from somewhere else.
I brushed my lips on her skin
and felt her presence through me,
her elegant containment
there in the cidery light.

THE FUTURE

The future, best greeted
without luggage in hand,
outside the terminal
where trees behave as they will,
dressing, undressing,
or dressed to kill,

where we are the species
birthing ideas
from our eyes from our hands
our ears our skin,
from soil in our pores
and love we pour out

in letters and emails—
the future is always
more open than we think,
though not for some,
the warnings remind us,
not for some.

Like you I am trying
to leave my luggage
behind in the car
or the circling carousel, walk
openhanded
from terminal doors.

Because like you
I have walked and flown
through calendar hours,

dreamed through minutes and years
and the breadcrumb days
I leave by the road . . .

We know we are nothing,
forgetting our names
or the names of the cities,
the nothing we know as we know
the light on a window,
river of rivers.

Out

When thunder tore the dark
I woke and smelled the rain
alone in another house
and all that held me gone.

I'd hurt you in the night
and left the day to bleed
and cast my self away
to chance it like a weed.

IN THE BARBER SHOP

The woman barber clips and combs and clips
a woman's hair, always solicitous,
touching her customer with utmost care,
while at the footrest a loving husband kneels,
consoling his frail wife in Polish, holding
her trembling hands in his big, clement hands.

Why is the wife (so thin and aged) afraid?
Why is the barber holding back her tears?
A stroke maybe? Maybe long history
related in those calming, murmured words.
And even if you've seen such love before
there's shame in having left it at the door,

in having thought too often of oneself
and present happiness. The husband pays
and wheels his whimpering, childlike wife outside
where winter sunlight strikes the anvil street,
and helicopter blades of light leap out
from windshields in the supermarket lot.

Now try to meet the barber's eyes, and take
your seat and let her pin the collar on.
Her touch, all business, has a healing power
but not enough, or not enough for you.
And when you pay and leave and feel the cold,
the dicing blades of light will scatter you.

Sarong Song

The woman in the blue sarong
bade me believe in ships.
Come sail with me, the journey's long,
sang her alluring lips

that baited me in a net of words
and hauled me to her bed
at the top of the world where thieving birds
loved me till I bled.

I came from an underworld of snow,
she from a windy dune.
She dared to look for me below
the phases of the moon.

Come walk with me, the journey's joy,
she sang with her blue eyes.
Untie the sarong, my bonny boy,
and bare me to the skies.

THE TARMAC

Lack, you say? The world will strip you naked.
Time you realized it. Too many years
you worked in a plush denial, head down,
dodging yourself as much as others.

Nobody did this to you.
Trained in deafness, you soon went blind,
but gathered strength for metamorphosis
in order to become your kind.

Now nothing helps but silence as you learn
slowly the letting go,
and learn again, and over again, again,
blow upon blow,

you must go by the way of mountain tides,
coral blizzards and the sunlit rain.
The wave of nausea heaves
and passes through the egocentric pain

and finds you on a tarmac going where
your skin and hair, eyes, ears and fingers feel
a change is in the air.
You are unfolding now, and almost real.

ANOTHER THING

Like fossil shells embedded in a stone,
you are an absence, rimmed calligraphy,
a mouthing out of silence, a way to see
beyond the bedroom where you lie alone.
So why not be the vast, antipodal cloud
you soloed under, riven by cold gales?
And why not be the song of diving whales,
why not the plosive surf below the road?

The others are one thing. They know they are.
One compass needle. They have found their way
and navigate by perfect cynosure.
Go wreck yourself once more against the day
and wash up like a bottle on the shore,
lucidity and salt in all you say.

LET IT GO

Earth, I walked on a trail of blooming dryad,
lay on a boulder, watching night come on,
the eager silhouetted limbs thrust up,
harmless night known first in a darker blue
then even darker to the dust of stars,
the far off traffic of a night-denying city,
the dogs calling, I thought, joyfully. Night,
harmless night when my love moves in her day
on the far side of Earth, an ocean away.

Today a friend called, his voice thick with grief
because he cannot stop himself from feeling,
because his joy and grief are the same chord
on the same bowed *lyra*. My friend is Greek, the *lyra*
no mere symbol but a mode of living, fire
in the night, cold water at dawn. And you, Earth,
have called out to us all our lives, in squall
and zephyr, flood and tidal wave, no one life
enough to hear the chord beyond belief.

Earth, I am learning mineral patience, moved
by the current of last night's dreaming, this morning's coffee.
Sometimes I hate you for coming between my love
and me, for being so large, so full of laws
and nations and money and people who cling to them all.
I know it is not your wish. I try to live
with animal resignation, grazing the weather,
alert for signs of danger. We've just begun,
my love and I, to meet beneath the sun.

We live each day in the shade of another life,
anonymous as all of space, or all
that passes under the canopy of leaves.
Earth, we cannot cling to you any more
than to each other. The life already over
is the one we love, the tears already shed,
the words already written, the magic drowned,
our feeling fire that sparks into the stars
while down below the ordinary cars

go on, abrasive and efficient commerce,
the houses glow and people lock their doors.
I'm shedding what I own, or trying to,
walking down the path of blooming dryad
and the pitch of pines, until I hear the stream
below me in the canyon, below the road,
below the traffic of ambition and denial,
the unclear water running to the sea,
the stream, dear Earth, between my love and me.

4 July 11

From over the ridge, chrysanthemums of fire
burst into color. One hears the pop-pop-pop
of another birthday, but the heart is flat champagne.

Who cares about freedom, and *Damn King George*?
Who cares about sirens out in city lights?
I've got enough to fight about right here,

the howitzer let loose inside my ribs,
the thudding ricochet from hill to hill,
from hurt to hurt. Hard birth. Hard coming to.

When I Didn't Get the News

I was on the Welsh coast, off
St. David's, on a bluff
looking down on the Atlantic

with Chrissy (chicken sandwiches,
strawberries and champagne
might have been the thing).

Instead, we drove
to the Snowdonian sunset
and returned to the full,
the rising moon.

I didn't get the news,
but slowly through the night
slept out the sweat of ages
channeled like a current over stones,

and woke to a day as calm and ordinary
as a blur of hedgerow,
a sunlit quarter of portioned field.

Small roadside phalanxes of foxglove
marshaled me to peace.

And that was when,
long after it had happened,
I did get the news,
or my computer did,

the simple fact that you were dead
and that I'd missed the whole final drama
while in my life.

The day of sunlight on the swales
and lowing cattle, glowing coals
of hillside sheep,

the day of fantasies about the perfect hovel
on the hill, the day we would try
to keep,

that day was the day my mother died,
simple fact—a useful thing, that—
and became *not here*

across thousands of miles of sea
and air.

I tried to think of who you were,
and how you tried to tell me at the end
to let go the whole baggage of the past.

No sense in grinding it to sausage,
no sense in cooking it to the perfect
killing meal.

The particular you, the wry jokes
and walking stick, the book groups
and bad girls who loved you—

might as well let them in
as they were the ones who knew you best,
the beautiful blind and halt,

the whiskey-soaked and all the rest
forgiven as they had forgiven you.

And I am with them too.

14 July 11

Where does a life go? Can't
answer that, can't go
where the holy rollers go.

I like the clouds, though,
above the hills at Brecon.
As trees are clouds,

as blown roses
and my love too, all cloud,
all rain, I reckon.

SALMON LEAP

The only constant was the sound of water,
and we, gill-breathing moss
and learning love would be there when we sought her,
prepared ourselves for loss.

Wherever absences are crossed by day
without a touch or look,
whenever there is nothing we can say,
remember the talking brook.

There is no deeper sleep than in the stream,
however it may fall
or heave in tides upon a distant dream.
Whatever voices call,

our ashes will be washed away by rain
and we will speak aloud
the language of a watery refrain,
clear as any cloud.

THE DYING MAN

After a week a man in a brown suit
appeared at the foot of the bed. They talked
a language of sunlight inside window glass
while family eyed each other wonderingly.

I also stood by the bed and held his hand
and brushed his hair and touched his beard.
He smiled and said, *No tears, but it's good to see
old friends.* In the kitchen women unwrapped food,

and in the garden everything was good.

The Insert

Change planes, change lives,
and why should any memory intervene?

The bridge you crossed
from school the day before you turned fourteen,

and found, behind
Bart's Mobil Station, two Lummi Indian girls

locked in a fight,
both grunting. One yanked the other's ironed curls

and tried to hold
her blouse together over heavy breasts.

Screaming now,
the other bled from nose and mouth, thickening gouts

that smeared her face
and stained the first girl's hands. You felt the hurt

and parted them
and stanched the bleeding with your balled-up shirt,

then walked away,
chilled in t-shirt, shouldering your bag of books.

And never saw
those girls again, except in sideways looks.

Change lives, change planes,
change anything you walk to or away from.

None of it stays
in place. None of it knows a trace of reason.

DIE WHEN YOU DIE

You, friend, have far to go. You cannot change
another and you cannot change yourself.
Let be. Weep when it is time for weeping,
laugh when laughter comes. No one else alive
will have a say in that.

                         Die when you die.

ONE ANOTHER

What current between us
touches abandoned days
to the present of yes?

Your face on the pillow
rapt in a distant glow
of self-loss, undertow,

drawn out deeper than love—
how will the days evolve,
the evenings believe

that what we are, we may
be without asking why,
given without a way.

As you are. That's how I
would have you be
if I had any say.

Leavings

How naked, how bereft
that wall of picture hooks
where faces used to make me cringe,
how bare the shelves
unloaded of their library, how like
another life the furnace
sighs to an empty house,
the decades it took a dresser
to leave its carpet mark,
its unvacuumed blur of dust.

Of six who lived here once
four are dead.
They've gone out before us.
I close the door, haunted.

LOPSIDED PRAYER

Bluejoint, fescue, foxglove, bee-sipped daisies
sign to the breeze what its direction is.

The night bleeds into everything you see.
Oh please be you. And please let me be me.

A Deafness

For days now at the mouth of the stream,
at the gray seam of gravel and sky,
a bald eagle has watched from pilings
kokanee moving inland to spawn.

The landlocked salmon dart past shallows
where he can feed, a lord at leisure.
They fan in alder-shadowed pools
until they die without a fight.

For we who cannot hear, this happens
with a more impartial love,
unruffled motion, like wet leaves
already fallen. No regret,

no whining need, no infant hurt,
nothing to say we're sorry for,
no chance to try again. A sinking,
used and belly-up in the stream.

And we keep going back to listen
through the moving shadows, the glide
and turn of bodies we have known,
to the deep evaders of desire.

THE SOUL FOX

for Chrissy, 28 October 2011

My love, the fox is in the yard.
The snow will bear his print a while,
then melt and go, but we who saw
his way of finding out, his night
of seeking, know what we have seen
and are the better for it. Write.
Let the white page bear the mark,
then melt with joy upon the dark.

Mrs. Mason and the Poets

At that point I had lived with Mr. Tighe
so many years apart from matrimony
we quite forgot the world would call it sin.
We were, in letters of our friends at Pisa,
Mr. and Mrs. Mason, the common name
domesticating the arrangement. (Our friends
were younger, thinking it a novelty.)

You've heard about Lord Byron and his zoo,
how he befriended geese he meant to eat
and how they ruled his villa like a byre
with peacocks, horses, monkeys, cats and crows.
And our friend Shelley whom we thought so ill,
whose brilliant wife was palely loitering,
waiting to give birth and dreading signs
that some disaster surely must befall them.
Shelley of the godless vegetable love,
pursuer of expensive causes, sprite.
He had confided in me more than once
how his enthusiasms caused him pain
and caused no end of pain to those he loved.

Some nights I see his blue eyes thrashing back
and comprehend how grieved he was, how aged.
Genius, yes, but often idiotic.
It took too many deaths, too many drownings,
fevers, accusations, to make him see
the ordinary life was not all bad.

I saw him last, not at the stormy pier
but in a dream. He came by candlelight,

one hand inside a pocket, and I said,
You look ill, you are tired, sit down and eat.

He answered, *No, I shall never eat more.*
I have not a soldo *left in all the world.*

Nonsense, this is no inn—you need not pay.

Perhaps it is the worse for that, he said.
He drew the hand out of his pocket, holding
a book of poems as if to buy his supper.
To see such brightness fallen broke my heart,
and then, of course, I learned that he had drowned.

Once, they say, he spread a paper out
upon a table, dipped his quill and made
a single dot of ink. *That,* he said,
is all of human knowledge, and the white
is all experience we dream of touching.
If I should spread more paper here, if all
the paper made by man were lying here,
that whiteness would be like experience,
but still our knowledge would be that one dot.

I've watched so many of the young die young.
As evening falls, I know that Mr. Tighe
will come back from his stroll, and he will say
to humour me, *Why Mrs. Mason, how*
might you have spent these several lovely hours?

And I shall notice how a slight peach flush
illuminates his whiskers as the sun
rounds the palms and enters at our windows.
And I shall say, *As you have, Mr. Mason,*
thinking of lost friends, wishing they were here.

And he: *Lost friends? Then I should pour the wine.*

And I? What shall I say to this kind man
but *Yes, my darling, time to pour the wine.*

MARCO POLO IN THE OLD HOTEL

Marco . . .
            . . . Polo

Marco . . .
            . . . Polo

Pour another glass of sunlight,
tasting an after-dinner hour.
This is not a time for reading.
Wait a while. A meteor shower
may fall about your head tonight
and children in a nearby pool
are laughing in late summer air,
happy to be free of school.

Marco . . .
            . . . Polo

Marco . . .
            . . . Polo

You are the only dinner guest.
The meal is finished, but the wine
will last until the dark arrives.
The children in the pool incline
their bodies, leaping from the waves,
their voices calling to each other,
traveling through the evenings, years
and decades of late-summer weather.

Marco . . .
                    . . . Polo

Marco . . .
                    . . . Polo

Across the parking lot a flag
is flapping, thin as Chinese silk
the camels caravanned through deserts.
Voices fall into the dark.
You breathe the last mouthful of wine
and seem to float into the air
as they call to eternity,
the un-enclosing everywhere:

Marco . . .
                    . . . Polo

Marco . . .
                    . . . Polo

A Sort of Oracle

Late one afternoon between sun and rain
I found the path ascending above Delphi
toward a spring an old man said I would find,
not knowing whom to ask about my life,
the wrongs I may have done myself or others,
and when I'd climbed beyond the yapping dogs
and the last engines of commercial traffic,
I asked an almond tree, an oracle
as good as any, for some forgiving word.

One does these things when nothing else makes sense,
feeling a giddy madness. The tree said nothing,
the cloudy shafts of sunlight stabbed, withdrew,
the cuckoo called from olives down below
its two comedic notes. I found the spring
and drank from it and washed the sweat from my face,
then turned back to the town where friends were waiting.

THE BAY OF WRITING

And I with only a reed in my hands.
—George Seferis

The reed, dried and cut, could make a pan-pipe
on an idle day. I say the word again,
kalamus, that early pen, from breezy
leaf to leaves of nervy writing—Sappho,
Archilochos, their fingering lines,
a silent music till our voices find it.

In retrospect I walk among those trees,
polled mulberries no longer home to silkworms,
the crone-like olives, upright cypresses
above the hammered metal of the bay
called *Kalamitsi*. There the lazy hours
watching the ant roads through the summer straw

taught me the frantic diligence of mind,
the way it ferries breadcrumbs and small seeds
fast fast to its storehouse in reedy shade.
The way the hand rests on an open book
I've disappeared into, takes up a pen
and traces letters in a trail of words.

Kalamus, *Kalamitsi*, bay of reeds,
music of everything I have not written.

FOGHORNS

The loneliest days,
damp and indistinct,
sea and land a haze.

And purple foghorns
blossomed over tides—
bruises being born

in silence, so slow,
so out there, around,
above and below.

In such hurts of sound
the known world became
neither flat nor round.

The steaming tea pot
was all we fathomed
of *is* and *is not*.

The hours were hallways
with doors at the ends
opened into days

fading into night
and the scattering
particles of light.

Nothing was done then.
Nothing was ever
done. Then it was done.

TREE LIGHT HOUSE

That slow familiar breathing
is the sea, I remember now,
and rain in the green limbs.
I dreamed your body
warm in the doona,
your unquestioning hands,
and woke to find you
fevered but alive
to be grateful for.

A cigarette lighter
fished from the surf
still lit the candles
at our little feast.
Night drew in
about the house
and when we fell
into bed the sea
erased our names.

The fever will not leave.
It will teach us waiting.
I write by the light of the trees,
by moss and salal,
the black flash of raven wings,
by the slow mist
salting the window,

rain on a neighbor's roof
reflecting.

Is it a form of prayer
or relinquishment,
this wish to be turning
away from tasks,
from the road with its string
of identical malls?
To be feeling again
the original touch
of the world?

When I was sick
my mother let me lie
about the house all day
and brought me ginger ale.
That's when I learned
by staying home from school
to live in the dream-time
as animals live
deeper in the world.

Your body heals itself
through fever,

the rasp of your cough
like surf over gravel.
Let me bring you tea,
let me feed you,
let me rock you
to the sweet
consolation of dreams.

We live high up in the trees
where bright green warblers rustle
and flit, songbeats in the light
and shadow. Where ravens sail
among the Sitka spruces
to rendezvous on branches.
We live in the breathing clock of the sea,
the whalesong of memory.
Wake me here. Lighten me.

THE BLUE OF THE BAY

What can be learned from the blue of the bay
I do not know, I cannot say,
the stone of the sand on the shore by the bay.

The bird on its back lying dead on the shore,
its breast torn open, its hollow core—
what more can be learned of the bird on the shore?

If someone is crying, I cannot hear,
and if I am crying inside I fear
no one will hear, no one will hear.

The moon held fast in the undertow.
I felt it pulling me, strong and slow,
the long withdrawing undertow,

and climbed on a barnacled rock by the sea,
the eelgrass wrapped around my knee,
my skin scrubbed raw by the cold cold sea.

If I can sleep I will dream of the day
drowning the hours in the deep blue bay,
the stone of the sand on the shore by the bay.

SEA SALT

Light dazzles from the grass
over the carnal dune.
This too shall come to pass,
but will it happen soon?
A kite nods to its string.
A cloud is happening

above the tripping waves,
joined by another cloud.
They are a crowd that moves.
The sky becomes a shroud
cut by a blade of sun.
There's nothing to be done.

The soul, if there's a soul
moves out to what it loves,
whatever makes it whole.
The sea stands still and moves,
denoting nothing new,
deliberating now.

The days are made of hours,
hours of instances,
and none of them are ours.
The sand blows through the fences.
Light darkens on the grass.
This too shall come to pass.

from ARRIVALS

2004

The City

From the Greek of C. P. Cavafy

You said: "I'll go away to another shore.
find another city better than this.
In all I attempt, something remains amiss
and my heart—like a dead thing—lies buried.
How long will my mind stew in all its worry?
Wherever I cast my eye, wherever I look,
I see the ruins of my life going black
here where I wasted and wrecked so many a year."

You won't find a new land or another shore.
This city will follow you, you'll molder
in these streets, in these neighborhoods grow older,
and turn gray among familiar houses.
You'll always end here—don't hope for other places.
There is no ship, there is no road for you.
Now that you have decided you are through
with this place, you've wrecked your life everywhere.

GULLS IN THE WAKE

Late in our journey from the pier at Kos,
I had come up for air. Most passengers
had found their bunks or drunk themselves asleep
in the comfy bar. Adrift and floodlit,

I let suspended time wash over me,
its kitchen smells, salt wind and plodding engines,
as two guys swinging beer cans walked the deck,
singing the liturgy. *Christ is risen!*

Drunken, genuinely happy, they waved
across cool space at constellated lights
of villages, and greeted me, a stranger.
I answered, *Truly He is risen*, though

I don't believe it. Not risen for this world.
Not here. Not now.
                              Then I heard cadences
of priestly chanting from an Athens church
broadcast to any pilgrim still awake.

Who could explain an unbeliever's joy
as rockets flared from the coast near Sounion
and music ferried death to life out there,
untethered in the dark?

And that was when I saw them—ghostly, winged,
doggedly following outside our light,
hopeful without a thought of hope, feeding
or diving to feed in waves I could not see.

KALAMITSI

A path I had not walked for sixteen years,
now almost hidden under rain-soaked grass
so even the locals told me it was gone,
but two steps down where it rounded the bay
and I was back. My heart beat all the faster.

Though half the olive trees had been cut down
the stone wall stood, the gate, the little house
looking as if no one ever lived there,
the cool spring where I dipped a pot for water
hidden by bramble mounds, the cistern greening.

I stiffly climbed the gate (now chained and locked)
and walked the point of land and knew each tree—
nothing but private memories, after all.
It wasn't the loss of time or friends that moved me
but the small survivals I was here to mark.

I had come through to see this much again,
and that plank bench under a cypress tree
where I had placed it all those years ago
to soak up shade on summer afternoons—
only a small plank bench, but quite enough.

PELICANS AND GREEKS

Edward Lear in San Remo, Italy, 1888

Nights when he cannot sleep, Lear looks for paper,
uncertain whether he should sketch or write,
or whether his living friends might comprehend
his travels off the rough and tumble roads.

As soon as I picked up my pen I felt
I was dying.

                    And should he then have married?
On such long nights, lines from the laureate
chase through his brain like notes flung off the scale—
an infant *with no language but a cry . . .*

What of Bassaë, the temple on the mountain,
the thickened oaks still stretching out their arms
to sunlight he had tried to catch in oils?
Who owned that painting now? How could one own
the love that lay behind it? All the years
and all the travels must mean little more
than light that dies along the temple flutings.

Laden with lunch, the drawing boards and paints,
Georgis played Sancho Panza to his knight.
Dear Georgis—you who witnessed wonders with me . . .
Spoken to nothing but an empty room.

On Crete a black man came, and little boy,
and peasants, and I drew them. They were all
good-tempered, laughing. I remember how
the small boy saw my drawing of a donkey

and almost cried and was impelled to give me
lemons as a gift. I gave him a pencil.
A gesture I can't forget, ingenuous
and awkward like the play of pelicans—
the ordinary beauty of the world
that makes one jubilate in sheer delight
and shudder when we feel life leaving us.

In India an English schoolgirl came
to meet the painter, having memorized
"The Owl and the Pussycat." Such was fame.
And there was Georgis who was mad again
because he could not ride an elephant.
And there were mountains higher than the ones
he loved in Crete and Thessaly. They too
compelled the draughtsman's longing not to lose
minute sensations he had drawn upon,
fleabags and palaces, pelicans and Greeks.

If no one bought my drawings I should live
on figs in summertime, worms in winter,
with olive trees and onions, a parrot,
yes, and two hedgehogs for companionship,
a painting room with absolute north light . . .

So many friends are gone. No partner frets
that he cannot sleep, no child arrives to scold him.
He is the sum of all that he has lost,
his hand still dreaming on the empty page.

Mumbai

The crowd's no apparition on Nehru Road,
nor the grit of motor rickshaws on Nehru Road.

Nor the steady pace of people, raga, rock,
and all the unheard music of Nehru Road.

Nor the flowers, the fruit, bowls of sacred colors,
the goats and cows that stroll down Nehru Road.

The tiffin wallahs, internet cafés,
the dogs that lick the pavement of Nehru Road.

The girls with perfect skin who wear their saris
with a demigoddess air on Nehru Road.

The crones who squat, the beggars, and the boy
washing himself from a pail on Nehru Road.

Commuters lean for air from open doors
as the long train leaves the stop on Nehru Road.

Mason, you've come to the other side of the world—
why can't you lose yourself on Nehru Road?

AGNOSTOS TOPOS

We had walked a whole day on high ridges
somewhere between the heat-struck sea and peaks,
each breath a desert in a traveler's lungs,
salt-stung, dusty, like summer's rasping grass
and the roughness of stone. Biblical thorns
penned us, while the stunted ilex trees
shadowed the path. It seemed from these dour fields
we could not emerge on anything like a road.

A landscape no one had commodified
or fenced. If there were gardens here
the poverty of soil defeated them.
If there were homes beyond some goatherd's hut
the gravity of ages pulled them down.
No sound but cicadas like high-pitched drills
ringing till red sunlight hissed into the sea.

And that was when, our shins scratched and throats parched,
we stumbled into a village on the shore
where people, stupefied by days upon days
that were the same, told us what to call this place.
The distance to a road? *Two cigarettes,*
said the old man who sat webbing his net.

Now the road cuts down from cliffs above.
I've been back, bought wine from the old man's son
who keeps his car parked in an olive's shade.
It's better, of course, that one can come and go.
One needn't stare a lifetime at hot cliffs,
thinking them impassable except to goats
and men whose speech and features grew like thorns.

The old man's dead. The friends I traveled with
are long since out of touch, and I'll admit
I've lost much of a young man's nimbleness.
I call these passing years *agnostos topos*,
unknown country, a place of panting lizards.
Yet how like home it seemed when I walked down
out of the unfenced hills, thirsty, footsore,
with words of greeting for the fisherman.

THE COLLECTOR'S TALE

When it was over I sat down last night,
shaken, and quite afraid I'd lost my mind.
The objects I have loved surrounded me
like friends in such composed society
they almost rid the atmosphere of fright.
I collected them, perhaps, as one inclined
to suffer other people stoically.

That's why, when I found Foley at my door—
not my shop, but here at my private home,
the smell of bourbon for his calling card—
I sighed and let him in without a word.
I'd only met the man two months before
and found his taste as tacky as they come,
his Indian ethic perfectly absurd.

The auction house in St. Paul where we met
was full that day of cherry furniture.
I still can't tell you why he'd chosen me
to lecture all about his Cherokee
obsessions, but I listened—that I regret.
My patience with a stranger's geniture
compelled him to describe his family tree.

He told me of his youth in Oklahoma,
his white father who steered clear of the Rez,
a grandma native healer who knew herbs
for every illness. Nothing like the 'burbs,
I guess. He learned to tell a real toma-
hawk from a handsaw, or lift his half-mad gaze
and "entertain" you with some acid barbs.

So he collected Indian artifacts,
the sort that sell for thousands in New York.
Beadwork, war shirts, arrowheads, shards of clay
beloved by dealers down in Santa Fe.
He lived to corner strangers, read them tracts
of his invention on the careful work
he would preserve and pridefully display.

Foley roamed the Great Plains in his van,
his thin hair tied back in a ponytail,
and people learned that he was smart enough
to deal. He made a living off this stuff,
became a more authenticated man.
But when he drank he would begin to rail
against the white world's trivializing fluff.

Last night when he came in, reeking of smoke
and liquor, gesticulating madly
as if we'd both returned from the same bar,
I heard him out a while, the drunken bore,
endured his leaning up against my oak
credenza there, until at last I gladly
offered him a drink and a kitchen chair.

I still see him, round as a medicine ball
with a three-day beard, wearing his ripped jeans
and ratty, unlaced Nikes without socks.
I see him searching through two empty packs
and casting them aside despite my scowl,
opening a third, lighting up—he careens
into my kitchen, leaving boozy tracks.

I offered brandy. He didn't mind the brand
or that I served it in a water glass.
He drank with simple greed, making no show
of thanks, and I could see he wouldn't go.
He told me nothing happened as he planned,
how he left Rasher's tiny shop a mess.
I killed him, Foley said. *You got to know.*

You know the place. Grand Avenue. The Great
White Way they built over my people's bones
after the western forts made stealing safe.
Safe for that fucking moneyed generation
F. Scott Fitzgerald tried to write about—
and here was Rasher, selling off such crap
no self-respecting dealer'd waste his time.

I heard he had good beadwork, Chippewa,
but when I went in all I saw was junk.
I'm thinking, Christ, the neighbors here must love him,
the one dusty-shuttered place on the block
and inside, counters filled with silver plate
so tarnished nobody would touch it, irons
with fraying cords and heaps of magazines.

He had the jawbone of a buffalo
from South Dakota, an old Enfield rifle,
a horn chair (or a cut-rate replica),
German Bible, a blue-eyed Jesus framed
in bottle caps—I mean he had everything

but paint-by-number sunsets, so much junk
I bet he hadn't made a sale in years.

You got to know this guy—skinny bald head
and both his hands twisted from arthritis.
I wouldn't give his place a second look
except I heard so much about this beadwork.
He leads me to a case in the back room.
I take a look. The stuff is fucking new,
pure Disneyland, not even off the Rez.

Foley's glass was empty; I poured him more
to buy time while I thought of some excuse
to get him out of here. If homicide
indeed were his odd tale's conclusion, I'd
rather let him pass out on my floor,
then dash upstairs and telephone the police.
I wouldn't mind if "fucking" Foley fried.

It's crap, he said. *I tell this slimy coot*
he doesn't know an Indian from a dog.
I can't believe I drove five hundred miles
to handle sentimental tourist crap.
He rolled himself upright in my kitchen chair
and looked at me with such complete disdain
that I imagined Mr. Rasher's stare.

I knew the man. We dealers somehow sense
who we trust and who the characters are.
I looked at my inebriated guest
and saw the fool-as-warrior on a quest

for the authentic, final recompense
that would rub out, in endless, private war,
all but his own image of the best.

Pretty quick I see I hurt his feelings.
He gets all proud on me and walks around
pointing at this and that,
a World's Fair pin, a Maris autograph,
and then he takes me to a dark wood cupboard
and spins the combination on the lock
and shows me what's inside. The old man

shows me his motherfucking pride and joy.
I look inside his cupboard and it's there
all right—a black man's head with eyes sewn shut—
I mean this fucker's real, all dried and stuffed,
a metal ashtray planted in the skull.
I look and it's like the old man's nodding,
Yeah, yeah, you prick, now tell me this is nothing.

He's looking at me looking at this head,
telling me he found it in a house
just up the street. Some dead white guy's estate
here in the liberal north allowed this coot
whatever his twisted little hands could take,
and then he hoards it away for special guests.
I didn't say a thing. I just walked out.

Now Foley filled his glass, drinking it down.
His irises caught fire as he lit up.
I sat across from him and wiped my palms

but inside I was setting off alarms
as if I should alert this sleeping town
that murder lived inside it. I could stop
the story now, I thought, but nothing calms

a killer when he knows he must confess,
and Foley'd chosen me to hear the worst.
Weird, he said, looking straight at me beyond
his burning cigarette. *I got so mad.*
Like all I thought of was a hundred shelves
collecting dust in Rasher's shop, and how
a dead man's head lay at the center of it.

I had to get a drink. Some yuppie bar
that charged a fortune for its cheapest bourbon.
I'm in there while the sun sets on the street
and people drop in after leaving work.
I look at all these happy people there—
laughing, anyway; maybe they aren't happy—
the well-dressed women tossing back their hair,

the men who loosen their designer ties
and sip their single malts—living on bones
of other people, right?
And two blocks down the street, in Rasher's shop,
a head where someone flicked his ashes once,
because of course a darky can't be human,
and someone's family kept that darky's head.

These genteel people with their decent souls
must have been embarrassed finding it,

and Rasher got it for a fucking song
and even he could never sell the thing.
No, he showed it to me just to get me,
just to prove I hadn't seen it all.
Well, he was right, I hadn't seen it all.

I didn't know the worst that people do
could be collected like a beaded bag,
bad medicine or good, we keep the stuff
and let it molder in our precious cases.
Some fucker cared just how he dried that head
and stitched the skin and cut the hole in the top—
big medicine for a man who liked cigars.

It's just another piece of history,
human, like a slave yoke or a scalping knife,
and maybe I was drunk on yuppie booze,
but I knew some things had to be destroyed.
Hell, I could hardly walk, but I walked back,
knocked on Rasher's door until he opened,
pushed him aside like a bag of raked-up leaves.

Maybe I was shouting, I don't know.
I heard him shouting at my back, and then
he came around between me and the case,
a little twisted guy with yellow teeth
telling me he'd call the fucking cops.
I found the jawbone of that buffalo.
I mean I must have picked it up somewhere,

maybe to break the lock, but I swung hard
and hit that old fucker upside the head
and he went down so easy I was shocked.
He lay there moaning in a spreading pool
I stepped around. I broke that old jawbone
prizing the lock, but it snapped free, and I
snatched out the gruesome head.

I got it to my van all right, and then
went back to check on Rasher. He was dead.
For a while I tried to set his shop on fire
to see the heaps of garbage in it burn,
but you'd need gasoline to get it going
and besides, I couldn't burn away the thought
of that weird thing I took from there tonight.

It's out there, Foley said. I'm parked outside
a few blocks down—I couldn't find your house.
I knew you'd listen to me if I came.
I knew you'd never try to turn me in.
You want to see it? No? I didn't either,
and now I'll never lose that goddamned head,
even if I bury it and drive away.

By now the bluster'd left his shrinking frame
and I thought he would vomit in my glass,
but Foley had saved strength enough to stand,
while I let go of everything I'd planned—
the telephone, police, and bitter fame

that might wash over my quiet life and pass
away at some inaudible command.

I thought of all the dead things in my shop.
No object I put up was poorly made.
Nothing of mine was inhumane, although
I felt death in a kind of undertow
pulling my life away. *Make it stop*,
I thought, as if poor Foley had betrayed
our best ideals. Of course I let him go.

The truth is, now he's left I feel relieved.
I locked the door behind him, but his smell
has lingered in my hallway all these hours.
I've mopped the floor, washed up, moved pots of flowers
to places that he touched. If I believed,
I would say Foley had emerged from hell.
I ask for help, but the silent house demurs.

In the Borrowed House

While flowerbeds have gone to seed,
a book you didn't plan to read
offers the unexpected phrase
that occupies your minds for days.

You write with someone else's pen
of someone else's life. And when
light's absence leans across the town,
you lay another body down.

ADAM SPEAKS

When I was clay there was so much to feel:
        symmetries of sunlight
traced within the feather and the leaf,
        pale secretions
trailing from shells, the clammy hands of fog
        touching my body.

My first uncurling into day was built
        from muted fires
below, and I began to grow distinct,
        bone, nail and hair,
muscled, akimbo, awkward as the fawn
        I later named.
There was a sea inside my flesh—I tensed
        to hold it in,
but found it was the whisper of the moon
        calling to me.

You who are thinking of me then, remember
        I tore my self
out of myself, bellowing like thunder.
        When I saw birds
I thought they were the love of God, and wailed
        at how they flew above me.

BALLADE AT 3 A.M.

A Dunkin' Donuts denizen,
Phil diagrammed conspiracies
in which the country had a plan,
contrived by top authorities,
to generate our mass malaise.
When I would ask him why or how,
suspicion flickered in his eyes.
I don't know where he's living now.

Jake had the presidential grin,
describing all the Saigon whores
who sold their wares to a bored Marine.
Due to his unexplained disease
he lived on federal subsidies,
though late at night he would avow
his fate was fixed by a hiring freeze.
I don't know where he's living now.

The bullet piercing Marvin's spleen
was not a North Vietnamese
but friendly fire from an M16.
He wasn't even overseas
and bore no combat memories
that might explain the way his brow
twitched as if he had DTs.
I don't know where he's living now.

Lost in the disco Seventies,
I met them briefly, anyhow,
and went on to my girlfriend's place.
I don't know where they're living now.

THE LOST HOUSE

A neighbor girl went with me near the creek,
entered the new house they were building there
with studs half-covered. Alone in summer dark,
we sat together on the plywood floor.

The sky way I contrived it, my right hand
slipped insinuatingly beneath her blouse
in new maneuvers, further than I planned.
I thought we floated in that almost-house.

Afraid of what might happen, or just afraid,
I stopped. She stood and brushed the sawdust off.
Fifteen that summer, we knew we could have strayed.
Now, if I saw it in a photograph,

I couldn't tell you where that new house stood.
One night the timbered hillside thundered down
like a dozen freight trains, crashing in a flood
that splintered walls and made the owners run.

By then I had been married and divorced.
The girl I reached for in unfinished walls
had moved away as if by nature's course.
The house was gone. Under quiet hills

The creek had cut new banks, left silt in bars
now sprouting alder scrub. No one would know,
cruising the dead-end road beneath the stars,
how we had trespassed there so long ago.

MR. LOUDEN AND THE ANTELOPE

Mr. Louden was my father's ranching friend
whose pickup sprouted rust from summer hail.
It didn't bother him. He had one arm,
and a tucked-in sleeve, and drove us toward the end
of his fence line, passing piñon and chaparral.
Forty years. By now he's bought the farm.

I can still hear him chuckling: *No, there ain't*
nothing funnier than a one-armed man
driving while he tries to swat horseflies.
I never heard him utter a complaint.
He could have been weathered sandstone, deadpan
when his empty sleeve flapped out in the breeze.

He released the wheel to point as antelope,
like dolphins of the desert that were playing
in our dusty wake, surfaced alongside us
and in one fleet formation climbed the slope
ahead, and over it. They left us saying
little and were far too fast to guide us.

Where were we headed in that battered truck,
my father, old Mr. Louden, and I?
And was it the hail-pocked wreck that I recall?
Now forty-eight, I can't believe my luck,
to have seen those agile creatures chasing by—
unless, of course, I only dreamed it all.

Though I can't prove it's true, I saw them go
out of sight like figures out of a myth.
They left us gasping in their kicked-up dust,

our own dust settling like summer snow,
while Mr. Louden laughed, conjuring with
his only arm, mage of the blooming rust.

A Meaning Made of Trees

From a phrase by Seamus Heaney

This bedroom high in the old house,
its roof pitched steeply overhead,

traps the lake water sounds, afloat
on what it holds: liquid lapping.

I could lie here half the day long,
hearing rain wrung out of the sky,

windows open, so the outer
breath and green of the world get in.

The alder's scabbed, serrated leaves
that will fail later in the fall

fulfill themselves, a waterfall
steeped in the greening chlorophyll.

That stir of limbs against the roof
must be the native Douglas fir—

a winter friend because it keeps
the housebound memory evergreen.

Most of all the cedar rises,
huge and straight, the hulking host

and omphalos of my dream world,
its rootedness a kind of triumph.

WINTER 1963

As my father turned the car into the drive
and we were home from our rare trip to church,
a man's voice speaking from the radio
caused us to linger there, engine running.
Just so, the voice with its calm cadences
lingered by woods where snow fell downily.

Though only eight, I thought I understood
the words to fit our snowless January,
and that the man, whose name was Robert Frost
(like rime I saw that morning on the lawn),
had died in Boston, which was far away.

Who knows where I went next, with all the woods
about the house to play in, but I recall
the chilling dullness of the winter sky
and firs so still I almost heard them breathing.
I thought it wasn't Jack, but Robert Frost,
Who made them live in such a cold repose.

Within two weeks another poet died,
her head in a cold gas oven. No poem
of hers was broadcast to my family.
Years would pass before I learned her name.

The old man in his woods, the young mother
dying with two babies near—such vanity
and madness framed the choices both had made—
the way he stuck it out, the way she lost it.

I've tried to cast my lot with that old man,
but something in her fate tugs at me too.
She can't have known the *cause célèbre* she'd be,
wanting to leave the world for leaving her.

The world goes on despite us and our poems,
snow falling in woods, or not falling,
lights coming on in houses, lights going out,
but I feel grateful that my father stopped
the car that January day, his head
almost bowed as he left the radio on.

SWIMMERS ON THE SHORE

Like half a filial circus act
splashing the Y pool shallow end,
I swam about my father, who could stand.
And when I climbed, an acrobat,
diving from his muscled shoulders,
they seemed as solid as two boulders.

Now I can hold his shrunken frame
in my arm's compass. We're together
on a park bench in lingering summer weather
before I make the long drive home.
But halfway through some story, speech
lies suddenly beyond his reach.

I see him cast for words, and fail.
Though talking never came with ease,
it is as if my father's memories
dissolve in a cedar-darkened pool,
while I no longer am aware
which of us goes fishing there.

Has he begun the long swim out
toward silence that we all half dread?
I hug my father's shoulders, lean my head
closer to his, yet I cannot,
from his unfinished sentences,
quite fathom where or who he is.

I want to stay. The day is warm,
the salt breeze blows across the Sound
long plaintive cries of seagulls sailing down

to hover over churning foam
there in the docking ferry's wake.
I want to stay for my own sake,

holding the man who once held me
until I dove and splashed about.
He gives my hand a squeeze. There is no doubt,
despite his loss of memory,
and though the words could not be found,
it's I who have begun to drown.

from THE COUNTRY I REMEMBER

1996

THE COUNTRY I REMEMBER: A NARRATIVE

The campfire embers are black and cold,

The banjos are broken, the stories are told,

The woods are cut down, and the young grown old.

—W. H. Auden, Paul Bunyan

How We Came This Far

Mrs. Maggie Gresham, Los Angeles, two years
before her death in 1956:

The rattle and sway of the train as it clattered across
leagues of open grassland put me to sleep,
and I dreamed of Illinois where land was flat
and safe as anything that I had known.
I woke to find my sisters counting bones
on the prairie, and the sky beyond our smoke
was a dusty blue. We were heading west.

Papa slept beneath his broad-brimmed hat
and Mama sewed—she made the pinafore
that I was wearing. I knelt beside my sisters,
watching land go by from the wooden seat
like waves of a great ocean being tossed.
The snow had melted, and everywhere it seemed
were bones like cages with no birds inside.

We'd packed a cheese, a stack of pies, boiled ham
and jars of fruit preserves from our old farm.
The Indians would come aboard each stop,
begging for food, or selling calico.
In Cheyenne my sister Beatrice had croup
and Mr. Kress said to take some snuff with lard
and spread it on her throat—that cured her quick.

I remember looking out the train at night,
trying to count the dark shapes passing by
and seeing our faces pressed against the glass
like children looking back from another world.
I thought of bones in the embrace of weeds,
of Indians who vanished on the prairie,
of hills that swayed and rumbled like our train.

Had my Papa brought us to this empty place
in desperation? I watched his regal head
nodding on his chest, the long V of beard
flowing over his crossed and worsted arms.
I was the happiest child when we had left
the farm, but now I prayed
the night would not destroy us like the lost.

The poets told us that this land was new
but, though I was a child, I understood
it was as ancient as the word of God,
and we were like those wandering tribes of old;
no one had chosen us to travel west,
and it would serve no purpose for a girl
to question choices that her parents made.

I knew this fear would always follow me
wherever I went, that I was not real,
that no one really lived who bore my name.
The lamplit face upon the swaying glass
was all that I would ever know of truth.
When Mama snuffed the lamp, my other face
retreated to the land of passing shadows.

Next morning while our mother brewed our tea
on one of the coal stoves inside the car,
I felt us being hauled away from dawn
by force of steam, and heard my Papa speak
to Mr. Kress of wars that he had fought in—
they whispered so we children wouldn't hear,
and Mr. Kress no longer looked so jolly.

The war that made my Papa look so old
happened in Tennessee and in Virginia
long before my sisters and I were born.
War had taught my Papa to stand up straight.
War gave him his heavy cough each winter,
but we had never heard the things I heard
intended for the ears of Mr. Kress.

Then the tea was ready and the two men
roused us children for another day.
They knew the reason we were heading west
and understood the bones out in the grass.
They were like prophets of the holy book
interpreting the tablets for the tribe,
and we the children of an Israel

unspoken for except by all the dead.

The Kresses said goodbye to us out West.
From Portland we went inland on the river—
strange to be pointed toward the East again
as if our path were the snake that eats its tail.
After the rivers and mountains of our journey
the land we traveled through was dry and grassy,
and Papa kept his stories to himself.

He paced the riverboat, nodding at land
because he'd known some part of it in youth
and memory had made him bring us back.
Washington Territory
looked for all we knew like the Holy Land,
and 1880 was our year of hope
and we believed our Papa understood

what made the wind blow steady off the buttes.

Papa bought the ranch near Pomeroy
and he had the first-ever frame house built
in the Blue Mountains, which were more like hills.
There the little savagery of childhood
ran its course—we tried to be young ladies,
but winters were hard; we had to dig out,
keeping an axe and shovel in the house.

Snow drifted over the fields and filled the lanes,
so Papa built a sled with a wagon box
and we rode to school over the tops of fences.

I had a dog named Buster who got lost
in a thick blizzard. Some of the men rode out
but saw no sign of him until that spring
a passing cowboy said he'd seen the bones.

Time passed. I thought of Buster on the prairie
and how we came this far from Illinois,
counting the bones beside the railroad tracks.
The snow had gone. The hills were turning green
and I was tired of all our little chores
on Papa's ranch, tired of staying home
with only a slow spinsterhood before me.

We came this far, and maybe I could go
farther on my own. Paper had slowed down
but wandering was in my blood—and his—
and he would have to understand my going
and how no place had ever been my home.
As long as I was moving there was hope
that I would find the place we all had sought—

even my Papa, back when he was young.

Cobb's Orchard

> *Lt. Mitchell shortly before his death*
> *at Pomeroy, Washington, in 1918:*

A hungry army's enough to spook the dead
the way it marches on without a sound,

only the clatter of our gear and wagons,
a noise of hoof and boot hemmed in by hills.
We were in McCook's force, pushing south,
the western flank of Rosecrans' three corps
butting General Bragg from Chattanooga.

Two days out of Goldsboro we ran short
of rations, feeding off the countryside.
The first day without food my boys made do
with coffee. After that my colored man
went out with a sack to gather what he could.
He caught up when we camped on Willow Creek,
a heap of elderberries all he'd found.

"We'll feast on 'em," I said. The 79th
had gathered hay enough for all our horses.
My company had elderberry juice,
cooked in kettles and coffee pots, for supper.
My Captain said, "Men, shake out your haversacks
for crumbs," but there weren't enough to feed a bird
and the men fell quiet, looking at their boots.

Charley was my colored man. He'd no horse
so I give him fifty cents to hire one,
told him to find our regimental sutler
back with the main force over the divide.
Next morning, Charley and the sutler came
right when the bugle sounded us to march,
and brought two wagons loaded down with food.

His people were still slaves, but Charley was free
and come to work for me not long after
we formed the 79th in Illinois.
The boys had voted me Lieutenant 'cause
I'd done a bit of fighting in the West—
bought me a fine sword I was proud to wear.
Charley kept it polished till it gleamed.

I meant to ask him where his people were,
but never did. He couldn't read a map.
He told me once he didn't want the Rebs
to catch him, fearing they would sell his hide.
When we got whipped at Chickamauga, Charley
had no place left to run. He just stood still
and waited for the Rebs to get a rope.

But all that hadn't happened when he rode for food . . .

Two more days with no supplies. We foraged
off the countryside as best we could.
I saw a Negro with his hat in his hand
ahead of us on the run. Charley and I
rode out to stop him. I wanted to know
what he was running from and if he knew
of anything out here to feed my men.

"Yes Suh," he says, pointing with his old hat.
He told of an orchard, five acres of fine
ripe peaches that belong to Senator Cobb.

"They's a rise and a ridge with a basin 'tween the two
   and right over that's a gulch and over that
   they's peaches enough for all you Yankees there."
I rode back and reported to my Colonel.

"Colonel," I says, "perhaps you can recall
   an ex-Senator Cobb who owns the land
   not far over that rise." I said I wanted
   men and wagons to feed the regiment.
He left me go with twenty-one infantry,
   an able Sergeant, sixteen cavalrymen
   for front and rear guards, the wagons and mules.

We found the orchard right where we were told,
   and I got the boys to cut their way to it,
   building a road so the wagons could cross the gulch.
We laid our ponchos underneath the trees
   and shook loose peaches so ripe you could smell them,
   filled two wagons, keeping one on reserve
   for any pigs or vegetables we might see.

It was a warm September day. The smell
   of grass and dust and peaches hung in the air.
Except for our harvest sounds, all was silent.
As far as we could see, no people worked
   the fields. All the men was fighting, I guess,
   and who knows where the women hid themselves
   with two great armies harvesting the land?

I took my mounted men across the hill
   to a large mansion, where I hollered, "Hello!"

A fat man stepped out who was full of whiskey.
"We have twenty-five thousand starving men,"
I told him. "If you have any food to give
I will receipt you for it. Swear loyalty
and you'll get paid."

                      "Damn your receipt," he said.

The boys unslung carbines to do him in
but I said we were only here for food
so let him be. The fat man cast an eye
up the ridge to my right, and there I saw
a mess of graycoats coming over the rise.
I give the order and we spurred our horses
down where my men had backed the empty wagon

to a corn crib. They had filled it with white corn
and I said, "Boys, the Rebs are after us!"
By this time I could hear their rebel yell
and thought a hail of Minié balls would hit us.
You never saw a mule team move so fast
as ours did, but I knew the Rebs were faster.
When we reached the road I had the wagons stop.

I had the teamsters run their mules to cover
and ordered the boys to line up double quick
in groups ten feet apart. The Rebs had stopped
on the hill behind us. I drew my sword
and let the sunlight catch it so they could see
the Yanks were ready for them. My Seargeant
was a big, hot fellow who wanted to fight.

He knew the Rebs could hear him so he said,
"You folks want our grub, you'll have to come on down."
We saw that they were not ready to come;
they couldn't tell how many men I had.
Our pickets had some trouble the day before,
so I said, "Boys, give 'em hell." I had them fire
four separate volleys for just three minutes.

The Vidette Cavalry rode up to see
our fight in time to watch the Rebs back off.
My men let out three cheers for the enemy.
Then we were on our way with wagons full,
two of peaches, one of corn and brandy.
The shooting warmed us up enough. I knew
the boys on foot stepped lighter than before.

Looking up, I saw birds fly between the trees
and disappear amid the tangled branches.
They seemed to follow us and share our joy,
lighthearted creatures made for a bit of song.
It took me back, I don't mind telling you,
as if this road led back to my family's farm,
turned west, and opened to the vast beyond.

But soldiers do like honey. At some bee stands
those who'd stolen a nip of brandy tried
to rob the hives. They had a worse skirmish
with those bees than the one with Johnny Reb.
You never saw so many stung-up fellows

raising dust as they leapt about the road.
I ordered a nip of brandy all round.

Half a mile on we saw hogs in the brush.
I rode to a nearby house and there found
an old couple dressed in homespun, sitting
in the shade of an oak. I asked about the hogs.
"Yes, Suh, we've seven if you count Old Betty."
"We have twenty-five thousand starving men,"
I told them. "I'll receipt you for those hogs.

If you're loyal, you'll get paid. If not,
you'll get nothing."
                          "Hell, Yankee," the old man said,
"I'm as loyal as you are. I love the old flag.
Mother and I just have to play rebel."
Mother said, "Let them Yankees have the hogs.
The Rebs will take them if you don't. Let them
have all but Old Betty, save Old Betty."

The boys went out and shot down six hogs,
all but Old Betty. I figured they were
two hundred pounds apiece, five cents a pound,
and wrote up a receipt for the old man
who touched my hand and wished me a safe journey.
Back then our farm in Illinois was much
like his, and it made me think of my wife and child.

We got back safe with peaches, corn, honey,
hogs and brandy, halted where the Colonel
rode out to meet us behind the picket lines.

"You have any trouble, Mitch?" he says.
"Yes Sir," I says, "we skirmished with some bees."
The men were a great sight, so badly stung
we had to laugh, but they ate well that night.

Some of the corn we cooked by laying ears
in the hot ashes of cooking fires, some
shelled and parched in the kettles of our cooks.
We slept all right, but next day had new orders
to cross the river and march to Sand Mountain—
we was on our way to Chickamauga.
Supplies were never sent to that old couple,

which has bothered my mind for all these years.

All Houses Are Haunted

Mrs. Gresham:

Some nights in the Palouse the moon-blue sky
was windless, stars adrift in its forever.
No one knew how often I left the ranch
and walked alone out to the luminous fields,
my nightdress trailing in grass like spun silver,
and lost myself in meditation there
before the day I really left for good.

When you leave a place it is more beautiful
those last few days, the earth will open up
secrets you never guessed at: the hushed grass,

the bluish cottonwood that seems to wait
and breathe with you in solitary union.
Alone on a hill at night, you can feel
the world was made for us to listen to.

Other nights I thought us the accidents
of a sorry God, or worse. Overcome
by silence, I could feel the planet whirl
like a crazy bronco bucking through space—
the best that we could do was grip the saddle.
Those were nights I felt I would be crushed,
my family would wake and not recall me.

Who was I but the girl who read Longfellow
to her Papa when his war-damaged eyes
no longer focused on the page, and when
no men came by to listen to his stories?
My sisters loved the poets too, but I
was the one who read aloud. I understood
always that I was here to be a voice.

"All houses wherein men have lived and died
are haunted houses." Yes, and looking back
across the fields, so wide awake around
my Papa's house, I saw how fragile love is,
how easy to uproot from any place,
how hard to plant again. I was a voice,
an echo, if you will,

though nothing echoed in that open land.

Acoustic Shadows

Lt. Mitchell:

We climbed Sand Mountain and could see the dust
raised by Bragg's army beating a retreat.
That night we saw the flash of cannon fire
but didn't hear a sound. "Acoustic shadow,"
the Colonel called it, hillsides all lit up
like summer lightning, but only a drizzle
hissed and the men were too dead tired to hear.

Then Bragg vanished. We were ordered back
to Chattanooga where we suffered more:
no rations, and water in short supply
so men drank from horse and mule tracks and wrung
out moisture from mud stuck to their ponchos.
Six miles out of Chattanooga we lay down
like dogs in the road beneath a long cliff.

More than a mile east, we could see a belt
of timber marking the river's course, the smoke
of rebel campfires drifting from the trees.
They had chosen this for their battlefield.
During the night we heard them move to the ground
below us, bivouac so near we smelled
tobacco sweet enough to drive us mad.

Next morning the big guns that woke us up
pounded a short ways up the line. Charley
brought me a cup of water he had scavenged.

"No more of them acoustic shades," he said,
and I could see he knew we were in for it.
The guns thudded and rapped like heavy mauls
driving a stout post deep into the ground.

I told the Colonel of a trick I learned
in the Indian campaigns out west. The men
could bite a cartridge end and suck a third
of the powder out. So stimulated then,
they would not think of their thirst. We'd be firing
at close range and would not need a full charge.
He sent the order out along the lines.

At daylight an orderly come up from Chattanooga:
"Men, get out of the road," he said. "No cheering."
Then General Garfield and his staff rode through
the lines, twelve officers who raised their hats
to every color they passed. They all set
forward in their saddles just a little
and made a sight. We formed ranks in their wake.

When my brigade come under enemy fire,
the Rebs shot from breastworks of brush and rock.
The 79th Illinois marched up
on top of them before we shouldered rifles.
We opened fire at thirty steps. Crazed with thirst,
our desperate men knelt down and kept on firing,
stood and fired again into the thick smoke.

We fought our way toward water, all our guns
rattling till they made a single roar,

Minié balls shredding through the grass and leaves
and boys dropping wounded to their knees.
we could see the timber belt, reached water
short of the river in a marsh. The men
threw off the scum and drank the puddles dry,

and found the spot alive with wiggle-tails.
We heard the rebels yell, and we yelled back,
though many of our boys were badly wounded.
For a moment the shooting stopped. My hand hurt
from gripping the sweaty hilt of my sword so tight,
but I was in one piece and saw to my men.
A fellow from Illinois fell next to me

and lay stone dead, staring up at the clouds,
blood thick in his beard. I saw where the ball
had ripped open his guts, and in his last
sad moments he had torn his tunic open
searching for the wound, now packed with dead leaves.
I just had time to dismount and close his eyes
and mutter a Lord have mercy over him.

But rebel sharpshooters lay ahead of us
on a hill, their bullets cutting through the trees.
Men were hit, horses were hit, and finally
a ball grazed Colonel Butler on the shoulder,
so he shouted to Captain Clark, "Get rid
of those pesky fellows, will you?" I told
the Captain, "Give me eight men. We'll climb up

that rock a quarter mile off and take
a shot at them." I got more volunteers
than I could use, chose eight from my company.
Colonel Butler said, "Mitch, dislodge those men."
I saluted and inquired of Captain Clark,
"What's your pleasure, Sir?" The Captain said,
"Kill the long-haired devils where you find them."

We pulled off our blue coats and haversacks,
  advancing from the Pennsylvanian line.
"Go get 'em, boys," said one. The Captain there
  only shook his head: "You won't come back."
At the base of the rock two poor skirmishers
  lay stone cold where the sharpshooters dropped them.
We crawled ahead, our pantaloons gray with dirt.

Then Tommy Wenn, a noble young churchgoer
from home said, "I'll pass over," and ran up.
The skirmish line kept firing to make work
for them sharpshooters, so Tommy could pass.
We all passed over in like manner, I last,
and with good cover climbed up the hillside
a mile, came out to the sharpshooters' rear.

They fired at our reserves a mile away,
  dropping bullets, you could say, from the clouds.
We advanced to spitting distance from the first
  sharpshooter. I told Tommy Wenn, "You wait
till he lifts up to shoot, then fire at him."
Tommy got the first man with a clean shot
through the head. We had to lay the body

over the splattered brains to hide the sight.
Tommy stayed in the dead man's barricade
to shoot the ground at intervals and fool
the Rebs while we went on to do the next.
We killed six in this fashion, with one left
atop a gulch. I took Jesse Peterson:
"Now Jesse, take your time, but get him good."

Jesse lowered his rifle and said, "Lieutenant,
I'm afraid my gun won't reach him from here."
We went further, till Jesse found a rock
to rest his rifle on. He cocked the gun,
and just as that rebel's hairy head appeared,
Jesse let him have it. We didn't bother
to gather up that sorry soul's remains,

but took the first six rifles back to our lines.
The soldiers raised Tommy Wenn on their shoulders
and gave three cheers for Mitchell and his men.
The colonel sent a dispatch bearing praise.
But while we did our job the rebel guns
blew up the roadside cliff two miles away,
killing some of General Garfield's staff.

I'd been in a shadow and I did not hear it.

Leaving Pomeroy

    Mrs. Gresham:

Running away is something children do
and I was not a child. Though I ran out
those many nights, I always came back home
by dawn to see to it that Papa was fed
and help out Mama any way I could.
She used to tell me I should have my own life
and there were plenty of men about who'd do.

My sisters snatched up half the able men
in Pomeroy. Oh, I had offers—eight
to be exact—but I had wanderlust
like some have measles. Anyway, my brother
lived for the ranch and would take care of it,
so I made plans to see my parents settled
and strike out for the world all on my own.

By 1900, Papa found the ranch
harder to manage. We bought the big house
in Pomeroy so we could take in boarders,
left the wheat and cattle in William's hands,
though Papa went back any day he could
to mend his fences or repair his tools
or just to wander in his memories.

Some people have no gift for growing old.
Though there were days my Papa could hardly breathe,
the old cough coming back, his eyesight poor,

though his hair and beard had long been white,
he still had the bearing of a younger man
and thought himself a soldier, and so his offspring
were forced to soldier with him all those years.

My sisters and I were quite small, like Mama,
with her brown hair and eyes, and some said we
were pretty, admiring our clothes and manners—
my parents made sure we were well-behaved—
and now with all the grandkids coming by
it seemed as if the Mitchell clan of Pomeroy
had justified their travels.

I was almost thirty. I had said no
enough to good men that my sisters thought
I'd lost what little brain I had. I helped
our Mama cook and clean for boarders, men
who came for harvest work, or to punch cows.
By autumn I had told them I was leaving.
Mama sat down, frozen in the kitchen,

and that night I made supper by myself.

She was ten years younger than our Papa was,
and a much sturdier Methodist than he—
she used to organize camp meetings back
in Illinois, and taught her children prayers.
The world we knew in childhood was all God's,

but somehow as we grew God slipped away,
or didn't hold us as He used to do.

The war hurt Mama too. Her brother died,
no one knew just where, and after that
her father had no use for Southerners
and never spoke to one. Papa, of course,
loved people no matter who they were,
wanted every stranger in Pomeroy
to stay at the Mitchell house and hear him tell

old tales about escape from Libby Prison.
My parents were so unlike each other in
the way they bore the burden of the past.
That day I took the train
I saw Mama cry for the first time ever;
Papa simply ordered me to write
and stood beside her, waving, as I left.

I see them both receding on the platform,
Papa in his suit and watch-chained vest,
Mama veiled as if for someone's funeral,
the whole town growing smaller till I saw
it wasn't a town at all, but a few trees
nestled in the grass of a great dry land
growing so much wider by the minute

that suddenly I feared what I had chosen.

Boyish War

Lt. Mitchell:

"All wars are boyish, and are fought by boys."
My daughter read that to me years ago—
Maggie, the one who left for California.
We weren't all boys. I was thirty-three
and I knew older men in uniform.
But we fought like boys. You know what I mean.
We bragged and laughed when we weren't terrified.

And I saw schoolkids torn apart by bullets,
their heads bashed in by Confederate rifles.
And I saw Yankees do a thing or two
to make those people hate us all their lives.
But in those days I couldn't waste my pity
on men who broken our union.
There was a fire in me that made me fight.

Not anger—no, nothing like that old Greek,
Achilles, who we read about at school.
I don't think I could ever really hate,
or could even understand Abe Lincoln's cause.
He was from Illinois and he was ours,
and we elected him our President,
and when he asked for volunteers, I went.

We was the right flank at Chickamauga,
and never saw the center of the fight
where Longstreet charged a gap in the Union lines
to give his West Point roommate, Rosecrans, hell
at great cost to both sides—many thousands
killed, wounded, or missing in two days—
and set the stage for Missionary Ridge.

After we killed the rebel sharpshooters,
my men and I stayed out on the high ground
for the view. We saw another old boy
dressed in a butternut suit, dodging and shooting
half a mile off, but didn't have the heart
to do him in. He only had a shotgun
and didn't kill a living thing I saw.

Near sundown seven stands of rebel colors
moved toward us from the Chattanooga side.
In the confusion of our fight that day,
as ranks were scattered and reformed in smoke,
the picture changed. I told my boys to move
back to the Pennsylvania skirmish line
as fast as their tired legs would carry them.

I told the Pennsylvania Colonel, "Sir,
there's seven stands of colors waving there.
They are for us, as we're inside their lines."
We found my Captain with the Illinois
telling the men tall tales beneath a tree.
In the dim light he asked, "Mitch, is that you?"
I passed him the bad news to give our Colonel.

Our order was to hold the rough terrain
at all hazards. The Army never thought
a Second Lieutenant could get tired or hungry
and I was given charge of Company F
whose Captain had been wounded in the morning.
I cast an eye for Charley, my colored man,
hoping he'd stayed arrears with our supplies,

but heard about his fate a few days later.

The land was full of hollows, broken fences,
and we moved like regiments of blind men,
blades before us, poking for the enemy.
Suddenly we was firing at their lines.
When they fired back we ordered, "Down to cover!"
Damned if they didn't pass right over us.
I ordered the boys to change, front to rear.

When we raised up I saw that we were stuck
between two rebel battle lines. The boys
in gray come running up and shouted, "Captain,
give us your sword."
                         "I can't see it that way,"
I said. A rebel parried, but one of mine
bayoneted him and was in turn thrust through
with a bayonet and dropped down at my feet.

The fellow who called me Captain bled and moaned
and died pretty quick. Though I couldn't see

a damned thing, I sensed the fight was over.
I slipped my sword inside my pantaloons
so when they captured us I walked stiff-legged.
A revel Sergeant much in sympathy
as me where I was hit and offered help.

I told him I fell off my horse and cracked my knee
and he said, "Suh, I b'lieve that hoss was shot."
Looking back, the whole thing seems unreal,
the way we walked along like two old friends.
Scattered shooting broke the night behind us,
though I could see that most of us were taken.
The rebels built a bonfire out of rails,

and in the firelight brought more prisoners in.
My Colonel hugged me like a baby, said,
"Mitch, you were worth your weight in gold today."
He said he knew that I could handle men
and would make Major if we could escape.
But we were told to sit down in the dark
and held at gunpoint all that weary night.

Next morning we were searched for valuables.
I hid my jackknife down inside my boot;
a ring I made from California gold
I wrapped in tobacco, pretending it a chew.
The officer in charge strolled up to me
and said, "Now I will have to have that sword."
He waited, arms crossed upon his tunic.

I didn't want to be dishonorable.
General Hull in the Revolution, who
commanded two of my own ancestors, broke
his sword in the ground when taken prisoner.
"I'm not going to make a Hull of myself,"
I said, but made no move to give it up
and offered silence to this officer.

It only made him madder. He detailed
three men with loaded pieces to take aim:
"Suh, I do not wish to use harsh measures."
I saw those barrels pointed at my breast
and thought of Mrs. Mitchell and the baby,
saw my chance for escape would have to wait,
unbuckled my sword and handed it across.

I felt just like twenty-five cents. They asked
whether my name was on the sword. It was not.
They regretted that it could not be returned.
I wished that I had given it to the rebel
Sergeant who saved my hide the night before,
but now I had to watch this officer
replace his rusty saber with my own.

Then I felt like six-and-a-quarter cents.

The Country I Remember

Mrs. Gresham:

By the time the train pulled into Portland, I
knew there was no one who could save my life
but me. Now I was twenty-nine years old,
a spinster with a love of poetry
and no money, experienced at cooking.
Portland was a brick city on the river
with some degraded shanties for the poor.

Fishermen, lumberjacks and prostitutes,
bartenders and bankers rambled her streets,
and I saw quickly it was rougher than
the frontier village that my Papa knew.
And wet. I swear it rained all winter long,
the smell of fish and cut wood everywhere.
I spent a week just wandering the streets,

looking for work to pay for my hotel,
but what could I do? I couldn't bring myself
to sing in a saloon with sawdust floors
or join the mission at the riverfront.
I saw that I had lived with family
to fortify me far too many years,
and I would have to learn to live alone.

The hotel keeper, Mr. Jenkins, must
have pitied me. He offered me a job,
first as kitchen help, then behind the desk

keeping his accounts. It paid my room and board
and something extra that I set aside—
my first Christmas away from home I sent
small presents to the folks at Pomeroy.

I had a private room on the first floor,
a bed and dresser and electric light
for reading so I didn't strain my eyes.
"It rains across the country I remember."
That was a line from Trumbull Stickney, read
in another room some other, later year,
but I remember feeling it in Portland,

closing my eyes and burrowing in the sheets
to listen to the water streaming down
the walls outside, the brick streets rushing
all that dark water downhill to the river
where it kept on going silently to sea
and clear across to China. I was alone.
I was alone and it was more than I could bear

to lie there listening to that driving rain.

Maybe that is why we go on talking,
always trying to show someone we're here,
and look—I have a past just like you do,
a stream of words that fills the empty night
and sweetens troubled dreams, or so we hope,
and tells us not to linger long on bridges
staring at all the water passing by.

I thought my whole ambition was to make
the past and present come together, dreamed
into a vivid shape that memory
could hold the way the land possesses rivers.
They in turn possess the land and carry it
in one clear stream of thought to drink from
or water gardens with.

I learned that I must first talk to myself,
retelling stories, muttering a few
remembered lines of verse, to make the earth
substantial and to bring the sunlight back.
I thought of all the bones out on the prairie,
or Mrs. Kress who came aboard our train
in a tight corset, so my sister Beatrice

said she looked like an ant. I thought of land
that flowed far out beneath us like a river
turning the dead face-upward in the wake
to talk to us of all their ruined lives
in a Babel of tongues. And then I knew
I worked to keep these troubled dreams at bay
and keep the talking dead from drowning me.

"It rains across the country I remember."

When spring came, Mr. Jenkins offered me
employment of another kind—a ring

along with all the duties of a wife.
He'd put his best suit on when he proposed
and I could see why others might have faltered,
fearing nights alone, but I was expert
at saying no and hardly knowing why.

I told him I would leave for California.

Sojourners

   Lt. Mitchell:

Some fella told me mankind always moves
from east to west, but in my day I've traveled
back and forth like a saw blade cutting wood.
When I was young I worked my father's farm,
but when at twenty-one I became a man
I left the farm work and the biting flies
to drive an ox team out to Oregon.

That was back in 1852.
The journey took three months, a lot on foot.
I saw whole households strewn across the prairies,
all extra furniture discarded when
we reached the bluish foothills of the mountains.
We added graves to those beside the trail
and traded worn-out oxen as we went.

At Cheyenne we picked up new wagon ruts
and followed them northwest across the hills

until high forests closed us in, the trail
full of growth we had to cut with axes.
I'd never seen such streams—what the poet called
"The cataract of death far thundering from
the heights"—clean as Heaven, shot with rainbows.

I'd say the mountain raised my spirits up
more than any sermon ever did.
I met a man who wintered there and looked
a granite carving brought to life by magic.
Everywhere I went I wondered how
it looked before it fell to human eyes,
before some storyteller called it home.

The mountains were home only to the gods,
according to the Indians, and I,
well I was young and I believed so much
the world was mine for taking.
                                    At last we came
to Portland, a town of log cabins then.
Never was a land so full of rain—
the ground soaked it up and squished when you walked.

The sky was always like a tattered mist
and most days keeping dry was hard to do,
but the woods was full of game, the lakes of fish,
and you could feed yourself with hardly a sweat.
I met a man named Barley who would fish
the river with a gill net like the natives,
hauling in salmon half as big as a man.

Joe Barley had come from Massachusetts
not for gold, but because he had no life
to hold him in the East. I fished with him
one fall, learned how to build an alder fire
and keep the coals banked low to smoke the fish.
I said I'd travel south to California;
Barley had a notion of coming too.

We panned for gold on the Humboldt, cut wheat
with cradles in the Sacramento Valley
the hottest month I ever labored through.
We packed mules to prospect in the country
near Mount Shasta and were lost for three days.
We heard about the Indian fights up north
and how the Rogue and Klamath picked a fight,

and then we joined the Oregon Mounted Dragoons
in 1856. They made us Corporals
and I recall my horse was so damned slow
I was always catching up. That's how I missed
half the fight in the Siskiyou Mountains,
rough, thick-wooded hills with lava outcrops,
where I saw Barley die, pierced by an arrow.

It wasn't more than three men we were chasing,
four months after Colonel Wright was murdered.
Some said Wright had raped an Indian girl,
some that she was the one who ate his heart.
A few of our men were still hot for revenge.
Barley, who had ridden out in front,
was nearly dead of bleeding when we found him.

They'd taken his horse, left barley in the sun
where we found him sitting up, swatting flies
and watching his own blood cover the grass.
"Mitch," he said, "I wish I'd stuck to fishing."
The Indians were hiding in the rocks.
Our men dismounted and were loading rifles,
shooting into the rocks, then running up.

The one they caught that day regretted it.
I was too busy holding my old friend
to notice all the noise on the hill above.
I must have looked up, though,
and when my eyes came back to Barley's face
the life had left it. I dug Barley's grave
and carved his name on a marker made of wood.

We had a preacher with us who could sermon:
"For we are strangers before thee," he said,
"and sojourners, as were all our fathers:
our days on the earth are as a shadow and
there is none abiding." He read some more
but those are words I don't think I'll forget.
They made me miss the farm in Illinois.

I knew my father must be getting old.

I thought of sojourners in the train's darkness,
hauled with other Union men to Richmond.
I fretted about the way I lost my sword,

and the stench of packed-in men hardly helped.
There wasn't room to tend the wounded ones
whose moans, together with the chugging train,
dragged through our days and nights of traveling.

The Chickamauga prisoners were kept
at Libby Prison down on Carey Street,
beside the James River and the Lynchburg Canal,
a brick warehouse built to hold tobacco
where now a thousand Union officers
huddled on its upper floors and learned
to sleep like spoons when nights grew long and cold.

"Well, you 'uns look like we 'uns, quite a little."
That was our greeting from the Reb commander,
pointing out his cannon aimed at the walls,
his soldiers eager to shoot all Yankees
attempting to escape. But I don't think
the man was evil; that night he fed us
beans and meat, never so much food again—

his men were hungry too, quite a little.

The Blacksmith

   Mrs. Gresham:

Howard Gresham pried a "yes" from me
by shear stubbornness. He was a strong man
and he simply wore me down. I'd lived alone

some years and thought I'd always live alone,
but fell for him as though I were a girl.
He wasn't a poet any more than I,
but he reminded me of some old verses:

"His hair is crisp, and black, and long,
        His face is like the tan;
His brow is wet with honest sweat,
        He earns whate'er he can,
And looks the whole world in the face,
        For he owes not any man."
Those were lines my Papa used to love.

Howard was a real blacksmith for ten years
who worked his way out west from Minnesota.
When I met him he owned a dry goods store
in Santa Rosa, where I worked as a cook
in a restaurant. He had these big strong arms
from wielding a heavy hammer all those years
and looked much like the fellow in the poem.

He'd come by the restaurant once and seen me
going in to work, and then he came back
and asked me on a picnic in the hills
outside of town. It was summer. "For lo,
the winter is past, the rain is over and gone;
The flowers appear on the earth . . ." Those words
were dancing about inside my head that day.

The hills of Santa Rosa had turned golden.
Sometimes they reminded me of the Palouse,

but winter wasn't hard in California.
I loved to take long walks outside of town,
so I said yes, and then I think I laughed
and said, "For lo, the winter is past." Howard
knew the verse and finished speaking it.

Right there is the restaurant that drew me
to him in a way I'd never felt before.
He knew the verse, though he'd had little school
because his father died at Gettysburg
and he'd had to learn a trade. I said yes,
I'd join him on his picnic in the hills.
That night I thought about it, doubts came back.

I told myself my travels were not done.
I still had thoughts of Mexico and further
south if money hadn't slowed my progress.
I had an idea that I would write a book,
but I could never sit still long enough.
I hardly knew this man, but clearly saw
that I could settle down and live with him.

No, I'd think, to marry him is to betray
yourself. Look at all the women you've known
who wear a path from house to school to church,
yoked like oxen, milked like cows, and told
to be as pretty as the foliage;
as if the noise of children's not enough
they nurse the manhood of their husbands too.

I ranted alone inside my rented room,
rejected Howard half a dozen times
when all he'd asked me was to go for a walk.
And when I tried to sleep I thought of love
and thought he would be capable of it.
And then: why would any man want me?
I'm such an old maid, thirty-six years old!

The picnic was a Sunday I had off.
We dallied for a long time on the ridge,
talking about our fathers and the war
and what we hoped for, coming west. I thought
the kindness in his face was kindness earned
by hardship and a solitude like mine.
He was forty-five and still a bachelor,

kept from marriage by his work and travel.
His family were all dead but a sister
in Minnesota he wrote postcards to.
For our picnic he brought sandwiches and beer
and threw a blanket on the grass, and we
sat in the shade of a black elm and talked.
When he returned me to my room that night

I had a wire that told me Mama had died.

When you have gone away to help yourself
a death at home is somehow more your fault,
as if you could have stopped it, made a mood

of happiness that would keep death at bay.
But I had not seen Mama since the day
she shrank beside my Papa as the train
pulled out—my last view of her, after all.

The train back home ran through the corridor
of rain to Portland, then by the river east.
I have never grown used to trains going east,
but the hills were familiar, farms of wheat
and standing herds out in the heat of summer.
All of my sisters were there, kids and husbands
with them, my shy brother and his new bride,

and Papa, standing on the platform, still
like a soldier, erect, his thinning hair
covered by a hat that matched his suit—
Mama would have bought him that and made him
wear it in the sun. He must have thought
she would see him buried in that suit, and now
sudden disbelief showed in his gaunt face.

Some of my sisters stayed at William's ranch
and let their children ride the horses. Papa
wanted me at the house in town, and said
he'd like to hear me read to him again,
which of course I did: Whitman on the war,
Longfellow and Lowell and Trumbull Stickney—
he liked that line of Stickney's on the rain.

Weather for a burial could not be found
at Pomeroy in summer: dusty blue

rose over the steeple and the grassy buttes.
"We brought nothing into this world, and it
is certain we can carry nothing out."
The minister was old, and his voice faint:
"I will lift up mine eyes unto the hills . . ."

The rustle of children filled the wooden pews,
and I heard their shoes on the floor, tapping
and scraping the Lord's floorboards, and I thought,
This is life going on, this is the form
of memory, the way our voices will remain.
I have avoided life too many years.
I have wanted to disappear, and now

at last I am ready for my life to come.

Rat Hell

   Lt. Mitchell:

The winter of 1863 and '4
was hard on all the men in Libby Prison.
Men from Gettysburg and Chickamauga
huddled on the upper floors, but when
we cooked or had our dead to carry down
the Rebs let us tarry on the ground floor.
By Christmas we were planning our escape.

Maybe you've heard of Colonel Rose's tunnel.
I was one of the fifteen men who dug,

sworn to an oath we would not tell the others
for fear the word would spread. If officers
escaped we might release the thirty thousand
private soldiers on Belle Isle, and then march
any way we could for the Union lines.

It was almost more than I could do to wait.

I knew a Sergeant Brown of the 25th
Virginia, came on duty at midnight, who
gave us tobacco and a morning paper.
A few years ago in Wallace, Idaho,
I met a lady in a bank who said,
"Lieutenant Mitchell, my father's an old soldier.
I want you two old veterans to meet."

I was in Wallace visiting a daughter.
One night this lady brung her father by
and I thought him familiar by his bearing,
and he said, "Yes, Lieutenant Mitchell, I
have given you tobacco many a time.
I was near court-martialed once for giving
a flask of whiskey to one of your wounded men."

If it wasn't Sergeant Brown! I visited
his home, and several old Confederates
come by, and we had a wonderful time.
We had a Southern meal in Idaho,
then cigars, and Sergeant Brown's daughter played

old songs we all knew on the piano,
as if no war had ever come between us.

There was a basement in the Libby Prison
called "Rat Hell," which was where we tunneled from.
In the Chickamauga Room we loosened floorboards,
slipped into the first-floor kitchen at night
and made a hidden hole behind a cook stove.
One of the men had rope and fixed a ladder,
sailor-fashion, for us to climb down on.

We dug out from the east wall of Rat Hell,
hoping to make it past a vacant lot
to a shed attached to a towing company,
our one tool the knife I'd hid in my boot,
a knife that still remains in my possession,
broken and mended, worn toothpick thin.
A hundred men depended on it once.

While digging, we could hear the guard above
in the lot call, "Three o'clock and all is well,"
and had to keep from laughing, though the work
was rough and the men who dug were all half sick
from the stink of the box sewer next to us.
By day we kept a watchman concealed in ricks
the Rebs had stacked below, and all day long

that fellow felt the rats run over him
and gnaw his flesh. One fellow used my knife

to kill a rat and baked it nice and brown
and said he never tasted sweeter meat,
it was just as good as squirrel.
                              Once the tunnel
broke a small hole into the vacant lot,
so I crawled in to see what could be done.

I'm telling you, to crawl under the earth,
smelling a stink that nearly made you sick,
inching yourself along by pulling roots
and wriggling like a worm inside a grave,
you can't lie still to think of smothering
but let your mind go blank and concentrate
on the job, like it's a piece of carpentry.

When I poked through to moonlight in the lot,
wearing a burlap sack we used for work
to spare our uniforms, I knew at once
I had to hide that hole. I scraped some mud
from the ground above and packed it with my blade,
making the airshaft look like a rat burrow—
so I hoped. Anyway, they never found us.

But I come out all mud from head to foot,
knowing I had caught a chill. Captain Clark
and Major Hamilton helped clean me up.
I donned my uniform and climbed upstairs;
by the time I found my blanket I was sick,
my skin all clammy and my forehead hot,
and knew that I had been that sick for days.

❖

I had bad dreams (and I am not a man
who dreams) of water boiling up from down
below, a shaft of moonlight turning it
to blood. I dreamed of cannon fire. One. Two.
The guns pounded like that. One. Two. Three. Four.
I saw my first-born buried on the farm
and prayed that I would live to see my wife.

I started coughing blood out of my lungs.
The rebel doctor said I had pneumonia.
When I heard that I thought I was a goner,
tried to sleep and stop the dreams from coming,
but when your fever's high like that, the mind
plays tricks on you. My breath came in great heaves
and the strangest dreams kept floating in my head.

The night they finished digging I recall
a dream of Mrs. Mitchell. As you know
she liked to keep things neat, and in my dream
she said I looked a mess. "Now Mitch," she said,
"you straighten out or I won't marry you."
I tell you, the woman never looked so fierce.
She frightened me so much I had to live.

"Now Mitch." It was the voice of Colonel Rose,
the night of February 9th. The boys
had thrown their blankets over me, he said.
"Now Mitch, this is goodbye. I hate to leave
a man behind, but you know we can't wait."

He looked a kindly bear with his great beard,
and I said I was glad to see them go.

More than a hundred men escaped that night.
The Rebs arrested their own guards, and would
have shot the bunch of them, but someone found
the tunnel, made a Negro boy crawl through
and saw where he come out inside the shed.
When they assembled all the men to count,
I was carried down cocooned in blankets,

and carried back, still moaning in my dreams.

The Children's Hour

    Mrs. Gresham:

This morning on the radio I heard
a robbery on Rosecrans Avenue
in Hawthorne got some old gentleman killed,
all for fifty dollars. And then I thought,
"Rosecrans Avenue," and it all came back,
how my Papa had fought in Rosecrans' army
at Chickamauga in 1863.

And when I was a girl I used to sneak
into the grown-ups' room, invisible
behind a chair, and listen to his stories.

Before he died a fellow wrote them down.
I have them in a box somewhere, with all
the letters Howard sent when we were courting
in Santa Rosa after Mama died.

No one ever wrote down Mama's stories.
And here we are in 1954.
I'm the last of the Mohicans, just about.
Ida died not long after Papa did.
Beatrice died in 1922.
Williams was killed by a horse in 1930.
Agnes died in a car wreck in Seattle.

Olive's living still in Pomeroy
and likes to call me on the telephone
to ask about the weather. She came down
to visit not long after Howard died
and went to see the houses of the stars.
My nieces and nephews are all grown up
and like to see Aunt Maggie in LA.

They say to grow old without children is
a curse, and sometimes I believe it's true—
to have so much to say and no one here
to say it to. I have a niece who comes
and takes me for a drive out by the sea
and shows me how the city's spreading out
clear to the mountains.
                              When we first came here

the place seemed almost as wild as Big Sur.
Howard had the store in Bakersfield
till 1928 when he retired
and we moved to Inglewood. All those years
we saw our chances for a family
go by until there was no chance at all.
Our baby didn't live beyond four months.

I tried to summon up my old belief
or find some verse that would relieve the pain,
but life won't always come when it is called.
We heard about the store in Bakersfield
and Howard saw the move would do us good
and I said, "Yes, my people always move
when staying in one place is killing them."

In Inglewood we used to have a shop
where we sold flowers, and I remember watching
young men stammer over roses for their girls
and thinking maybe I had let it all
go by too quickly. I had some regrets,
wondering if old age would be as dry
and dusty as the hills.

Depression, war, rations and hard times.
Howard wouldn't let me dwell in the dark.
That's what we had work and laughter for,
he said, to pull us out and land us on
our feet, and keep our dead from sinking us.
He was like Papa in that way, knowing
always how to plant his feet on the ground.

The other day my niece, Alyssa, brought
her two young girls along and we had dinner
near Pacific Avenue, then drove out
to the beach where the girls could have a swim.
They were such lovely things, with their long hair
and much more freedom than I ever knew,
the way they flirted with the boys out there.

Alyssa rambled on about her job
selling real estate after her divorce,
and while I listened, all at once I heard
the hoofbeats of the surf come pounding in.
I thought it was the voice of memory
crashing and flowing down across the earth,
and underneath, like roots that probe for water,

and I was moved by everything that moved.

Eighty Acres

   Lt. Mitchell:

In 1866 my son was born,
William Thomas, partly named for the Rock
of Chickamauga. My father, getting old,
wanted me to stay on and care for him,
so I built a good frame house next to his
and worked our eighty acres in Edgar County,
and raised my children up with Mrs. Mitchell.

We'd cattle and fowl, corn and timothy.
The children walked two miles to school, and had
a fine teacher who taught them proper speech.
I like people, as you know. Anyone
passing by was invited in to dinner.
One time a walleyed man and his daughter passed
and stayed for three years, helping on the farm.

The daughter taught my girls to sing folk songs:
"Froggie Went A-Courtin'," "Little Brown Jug."
In 1876 my uncles come
to see my father once before he died.
He was ninety then, but when they arrived
he rose from bed he was so glad to see them.
My father died in 1878.

Mother had passed on twenty years before.
I was damn near fifty myself, and saw
it might be my last chance to move out West.
This country's always on the move. Sometimes
if you don't want to carry a great weight
you drop it and walk away. America's
made up by those who want to change themselves—

my father did the same when he come out
from Boone County, Kentucky, years before.
Now my wife was thirty-nine, but healthy.
we sold the farm with all our furniture
at auction, tools I sometimes wish I'd kept,
loaded up our five daughters and one son
and took the train from Paris, Illinois.

That was the last my wife saw of her folks.

They kept me seven months in Libby Prison,
part of the time so sick I thought I'd die,
the rest malnourished, hardly able to walk.
The Rebs recaptured nearly half the men
who crawled out through the tunnel. Some they kept
below in cages where they fed on rats.
The whole business was a bit discouraging.

The more the war went on the meaner it got,
and we were glad to hear the Union guns
start in on Richmond. One day a Reb guard
come upstairs where we were sitting, and said,
"What are you boys doing?" He looked half crazed.
I told him that as far as I could tell
we were prisoners of war. He was new,

just a kid, looking at us lying there:
"You fellas ever get anything to eat?"
I said we had a ration every day
and it was pretty good but not enough.
There was a bucket of beans and some cornbread
brought up, and the boy look at it and said,
"Is that the kind of stuff you have in here?"

He said he wouldn't touch it for it was full
of worms. I told him, "I don't see no worms."
I ate my ration, but the rebel boy

wouldn't eat. Next day I guess he was hungry
and he said he couldn't see no worms either.
The Confederates there ate the same rations
we did, just like they were prisoners too.

A whole mess of new prisoners arrived,
but Richmond was done for. They lined us up
outside, where I stood a while in the shade.
A chaplain come up and said, "Lieutenant Mitchell,
why don't you fall in line?" I said the ground
was too rough for me to walk upon. "Why,"
he says, "it's level as a floor out here."

But to me the whole city seemed to wobble.

They shipped us first to Macon, Georgia, then
to the jail yard in Charleston, South Carolina,
where we saw Union batteries lobbing shells
into the burning city; so they pulled us out,
giving us rice and cabbage leaves to eat,
to a place called Camp Sorghum, near Columbia.
I don't mind telling you conditions there was bad.

More sick and crippled men I'd never seen,
and many died. Some days I felt oppressed.
It seemed that if we stayed there we would die.
When I think back to all those muddy graves,

sometimes I recall a line of poetry
my daughter read to me: "O how can it be
that the ground does not sicken?"

The world was sick and winter on its way.

Maybe the Rebs were just too tired to watch us.
One night half a dozen of us bolted,
struck out across a field that once had been
full of cotton, for you could see the rows,
and into trees that scattered water on us.
It was damn foggy and we ran all night
only to find we'd circled back to camp!

So we started the opposite way and come
to a house with a lady out fetching water.
One of the men had a gray suit and went
to her and said he was Confederate,
and she said, "I will divide what I have
with a Confederate soldier," and gave
him biscuits which he carried back to us.

While he was in the house a sow come by
with four or five pigs. I was accurate
with a rock, but I threw and threw at those pigs
and never hit a one. I couldn't see
distinctly anymore from months of hunger.
We walked at night without a star for guide
till we saw there was someone on the trail:

a Negro wandered along on his way back
to a camp where he was working as a cook.
We told him we were Yanks and he was scared
but said, "God bless," and took us to his cabin.
His people there had little food, but gave us
bacon and cornbread, let us get some sleep.
They said we had been moving south and might

catch up with General Sherman in Augusta,
sixteen miles away. For men as tired
and worn out as we were, that was good news.
In all my rambling days I never felt
a sixteen miles so distant. We left at daybreak
so we could see our route across a swamp,
threw our shoes away as they were almost gone,

and made ourselves some moccasins from the hide
of a dead cow we found mired in the mud.
But we would never make it to Augusta.
We ran straight into a rebel picket line
where Morgan's men were shouting, "Halt. Halt. Halt."
One was so excited his rifle shook
at us and I thought he would shoot. He said,

"Give us fair play, Yankees, give us fair play."

This is an account of my experience,
though much is left out: the end of the war
and sorry death of Mr. Lincoln, months

in hospitals getting my strength back,
return to Edgar County, Illinois,
where Mrs. Mitchell, who had had no news
for quite a time, was glad to see me home.

I had little enough to show her for
the trouble of my being gone. The sword
I bought in Washington for the last parade
was not as fine as the one that I had lost
at Chickamauga. She told me our first-born
died while I was gone. No one knew the cause
and she had kept her grief for my return.

I've told these tales before, but wanted someone
to set them properly on paper, now,
in case my mind in old age starts to drift.
They say that when you age the distant things
are closest, and some days I find that true.
Sometimes I think of Oregon and young
Joe Barley, and the lonely way he died.

Sometimes I think of all the blood we've spilled,
but thinking that way only brings bad dreams.
It's good to have the young ones dropping by
for visits, though Maggie never had her own
and she's still living out in California.
Mrs. Mitchell died twelve years ago.
It come sudden. The doctor said a stroke.

Forty-eight years together, she and I,
and most of it was work. A fellow can't

put into words the help she gave us all.
Not only the children. There were bad days
glumness got the better of me, she said,
"Mitch, you've come too far to give up now."
I talk a lot, but some things I can't say.

I'm getting used to living here in town.
This is my home. This is my home because
I say it is. I told you about my life
so you would know how this place is my home.
I knew I'd come back like a boy in love
and build my wife that frame house, room by room.
I knew that one of us would choose a grave.

And I will rest there when my time has come.

In the Northern Woods

The wind that stripped the birches by the lake
dusted the first snow on her hollow gaze,
then warmed her slender limbs for no one's sake.
Hunters who found her stood by in a daze,
kerchiefs on faces, till the sheriff came.
No records ever gave the girl a name.

Anonymous as leaves along the shore,
where waves fall into lines until they freeze
and winter drifts against a cabin door
and change comes quickly on a southern breeze,
the birds will tell us nothing of her worth
whose small bones left no imprint on the earth.

SONG OF THE POWERS

Mine, said the stone,
mine is the hour.
I crush the scissors,
such is my power.
Stronger than wishes,
my power, alone.

Mine, said the paper,
mine are the words
that smother the stone
with imagined birds,
reams of them flown
from the mind of the shaper.

Mine, said the scissors,
mine all the knives
gashing through paper's
ethereal lives;
nothing's so proper
as tattering wishes.

As stone crushes scissors,
as paper snuffs stone
and scissors cut paper,
all end alone.
So heap up your paper
and scissor your wishes
and uproot the stone
from the top of the hill.
They all end alone
as you will, you will.

A MOTION WE CANNOT SEE

We found the path somewhat as it had been:
heather and rock of an alpine meadow
ringed by peaks like giants in a myth
we never learned; all our lives
we had played among them, and perhaps
our grief was payment of an unknown debt.

Perhaps the strange mist
caused us to question the path,
but our boots made a familiar sound
on the dirt runnel; the gray rocks
and stunted firs were congregated
as before.

We couldn't say why we had come,
two living brothers and our father
whose hands were like ours
and like our brother's hands,
bones and hair so much like ours,
flesh of our silent flesh.

I saw the place where we had cupped
the ashes, letting them blow
and drift over the heather.
A year of snow and snowmelt later
what could be left of him,
so utterly possessed by mountains?

Yet after a year of weather
tiny pieces of my brother's bone
still lay in clefts of rock.

We found them under our hands,
cupping them once again in wonder
at what the giants left us.

Since then I have not gone back
to hold my brother's bones. The prayers
of blizzard and snowmelt have him now,
and time flows down the mountain like the ice,
a motion we cannot see,
though it bears our blood almost forever.

THE SOCKEYE

Two Aleut boys, poles sawed off for work,
run along the banks, over keels and gunwales
of dragged-up skiffs, following the ripples
for shadows of a fin;
the submerged eyes intent on dreaming home
under the shirring water, under the clouds,
the life swimming inland,
hooked suddenly and fought up the steep bank,
a saw-mouthed sockeye flips on the wet stones
until they club it and slit its belly open.

All my life I have tried to make sense
of what I cannot see. Those days alone
I thought I was close to it, swimming freely
under the watery clouds. Then I was hooked
and flapping, exposed to another sky.
Still being human, I wanted to dissolve,
to escape beyond my limited knowledge
of blank hills and riprap, road and gull cry,
to swim out further than I knew, and find
the skill of children fishing on a river.

ON BEING DISMISSED AS A PASTORAL POET

The mounds of pocket gophers punctuate
these prairie stutterings of growth: willow
and poplar and cottonwood, bluestem grass—
and look, a little slip of a cowslip pokes
up from the muddy fringes of a creek.
The market value of such local knowledge
plunges yearly to new depths—one's failure
to sophisticate these vast edges drear
with monologues on God's withdrawing roar
(for all I know, She hasn't arrived yet).

No shepherd parks his flock in this here field
and over yonder cash is all they grow.
The only oaten reed or reedy oat
I know's the railroad's melancholy note—
the train wails by ten times a day and traps
the traffic between Target and Cash Wise.
The eclogues you despise are hard to write.
Should I apologize for small-town ways
that offer to the critic nothing new?
Well, let me add what Mrs. Ferndale says,

counting train cars: "Fuck you, fuck you, fuck you . . ."

from THE BURIED HOUSES

1991

GUSEV

from the story by Anton Chekhov

The wind has broken free of its chain.
The sea has neither sense nor pity,
and what befalls us falls like rain.
The water's hot as new-made jelly.

The sea has neither sense nor pity.
One dies while playing a game of cards.
The water's hot as new-made jelly.
Above it there are curious clouds.

One dies while playing a game of cards.
Pavel insists he is getting well.
Above the ship are curious clouds
like lions leaping over the swell.

Pavel insists he is getting well
and dies despising the peasant class.
Lions leaping over the swell
turn to scissors as they pass.

He dies despising the peasant class
while Gusev lies in a fevered state.
Clouds turn to scissors as they pass
and dead men find it hard to hate.

Gusev lies in a fevered state,
wishing he didn't have to die,
and though he finds it hard to hate
he's saddened when he sees the sky.

Wishing he didn't have to die,
he goes below to suffocate,
saddened now he's seen the sky.
He thinks of snow, the village gate,

and goes below to suffocate,
his dreams increasingly absurd.
he sleighs through snow, the village gate,
sleeps two days, dies on the third.

His dreams increasingly absurd,
he tosses the fever from his bed,
sleeps two days, dies on the third.
They sew the sail cloth over his head.

He tosses the fever from his bed.
the fever smiles and crawls back in.
They sew the sail cloth over his head.
Below deck someone's dying again.

The fever smiles and crawls back in.
The wind has broken free of its chain.
Below deck someone's dying again,
and what befalls us falls like rain.

THE NIGHTINGALES OF ANDRÍTSENA

What did my young compatriots think of me,
those fawn-skinned children blond as German beer,
or the dark-haired ones full of their own freshness?
Did they wonder how I came to live in Greece,
or was I simply Mrs. Finn—translator,
tour guide, sadly middle-aged? As agreed
we met in Athens, and our Arcadian sweep
through history in an air-conditioned bus
began.

            Professor Baird was keen to know
the right way to pronounce Epídauros.
At Nestor's Palace he lectured out on the grass,
but those of us who formed his audience
were dazzled by the sea, the fishing boats
caught, it seemed, in pure, unframeable blue.
Though I sat politely, hands in my lap,
the students might have seen I hated lectures.
Perhaps they didn't notice me at all,
and who could blame them? Why should they want to know
one's hair grays, one's husband leaves, one's tongue
turns to stone?

            My children, older than these,
live in America. I have a room
on Skyros facing the sea, a single bed.
I read long books alone just as I did
that night in Chicago many years ago
they came to tell me that my father was dead.

I have no reason to keep living here—
not a real one. It's better for these students
wanting sunlight and a good rate of exchange.

For some it's always harder. They want more
but with a vague unease, as I wanted words
to guide me by the solid things they stood for,
held like the tang of wine, tasted like flesh,
as if all time might coalesce, memorable,
firm and rounded by the motions of the sea.

One boy, Ross, was like that. He had come
from a small town near Seattle. Reading books
had given him his first whiff of the world.
I think he was nineteen. I remember thinking
Oh, to be nineteen again, blessedly
empty-headed, able to dream in Greek!
He was the only student on the bus
who wanted lessons; for him the language came
like something his body's motion could inhabit.

A girl named Angela would sit near Ross.
I thought them a couple, as we often do
who watch young people from a distance, guessing
at their lives. Both were good-looking, dark-haired,
with burnished faces, dreamy more than studious.
But he was curious—about the world, I mean—
and that set him apart. Angela, I think,
was curious about Ross.

We became friends.
The girl joined us at our breakfast lessons,
fumbled with us through the primer, as if
our struggle with words puzzled and intrigued her.
I didn't mind. He wasn't distracted yet.

We left the seacoast with its olive groves,
its sunlit trellises, baskets of fish
and bougainvillea. Our bus turned inland.
Above Andrítsena the Temple of Bassaë
crowned its grassy mountain, the gray stone
columns weathered more than the Parthenon's,
each of them set apart like a new word,
magnificent in mass and workmanship.

After the usual lecture professor Baird
took most of his charges back to the hotel.
Ross and Angela lingered behind with me;
the keeper showed us how to find the path.
"Walking is good for the heart," the keeper said,
though he was waiting for his cousin's taxi.

Good for the heart, the silence after lectures,
after the last black spume of bus exhaust,
the silence of a walk through oak forests.
Ross was the strongest of us, but held back,
letting me set our pace. He wanted to know
the words for temple, footpath, oak, stream.
Here the trees were large and very old.

We heard the tuneless clatter of goat bells
and saw the shepherd watching from his ridge.

We saw Andrítsena from above, came down
as if to land like birds on its tiled rooftops.
The paths were full of wood smoke, cooking smells
that quickened us. We had come eight miles
in near silence; the chatter of village life
rose slowly as we entered and sat down
under the plane tree by the cistern. Ross
opened the cistern's door, described its room
carved out of rock, full of the cool water.
His voice became two voices, one loud
and hollow like a cave, the other muted,
ordinary, as he withdrew his head and laughed.
But we couldn't linger there. We were late
to meet the others at the tourist hotel.

The nightingales won't let you sleep in Platres.

Sitting on my balcony as evening drifted
down from the oak forests, from the strong limbs
of the gray temple, into the gully below,
I had opened my Seferis to that poem.

Won't let you sleep, won't let you sleep. The day
had filled me with its grand foolishness,
being caught up by, of all things, a rhythm.
Won't let you sleep.

So, you must be thinking,
here comes the epiphany of Mrs. Finn,
the moment when she sees how vain she is,
and you won't be far from wrong. I sat alone,
wondering what they thought of me, but mostly
what he thought, younger than my youngest son.
Hadn't my husband done it, chased the body
of a girl he hardly knew, someone met
at work, a plaything he later bored?

I knew that soon Ross and Angela would come
and we would listen for the nightingales.
The maid had told us there were nightingales
capable of twelve distinctive melodies.
Imagine that—twelve songs by heart, and all
the literary baggage: Keats, Seferis . . .

I sat there frozen, holding my Seferis
and thinking how they wouldn't let me sleep,
the images, that girl reading her book
in Chicago when they came with the awful news.
I held the book so tightly in my lap
that I had bent its cover.

The children came. I saw that they were children
in spite of their gracious manner with the wine.
They both wore shorts. I admired their brown limbs,
saw the gentle way he touched her hand.

At last we heard the singing from the shadows
of the dark, silent chorus of the leaves.

We listened for the life inside each note,
or rather the children did, Ross leaning
out as if resisting an urge to fly;
Angela, her sense of possibility
untarnished, smiled like an archaic statue.

For me it had all gone flat. I won't deny
the music of the birds was beautiful,
but I saw how we transformed it in our minds
to what we had expected it to be.
I saw the evening's mood envelope them,
how what they had desired became a shell
of words—of empty, captivating words.

It angered me that I could think this way.
I knew that I was spiteful, that the girl
had everything I thought I'd ever wanted,
the thoughtlessness that comes with being young.

Because of who I am, who I've always been,
I know the nightingales won't let me sleep.
I do not think I have ever been young.
I do not think I have let myself be young.
I am a woman whose father committed suicide
in Chicago in 1939.

At the Graves of Castor and Pollux

It breaks your back
to consider the stones
men used to bear,
not to mention
their burden of belief.
The constellations
animated

guards against loss,
guiding sailors home.
We are meant to believe
of Leda's sons
that the wrestler was a midget
and lay with his brother
in these chiseled troughs.

Brothers who fought,
scaling Taygetus
on a worn path
above the trees
to the bluest death,
the farthest arch,
Gemini.

I dreamed
a hall light was on,
my own brother
coming to see me
months after he fell.
I was never happier,
shouting his name that was

palpable as a shell.
In the old days
dead men were seen
in the stars,
courses charted,
walls built . . .
I'll watch tonight.

SPOONING

After my grandfather died I went back
to help my mother sell his furniture:
the old chair he did his sitting on,
the kitchen things. Going through his boxes
I found letters, cancelled checks, the usual
old photographs of relatives I hardly knew
and Grandmother, clutching an apron in both hands.

And *her*. There was an old publicity still
taken when she wore her hair like a helmet,
polished black. Posed before a cardboard shell
and painted waves, she seemed unattainable,
as she was meant to.

                    For years we thought he lied
about his knowing her when he was young,
but Grandfather was a man who hated liars,
a man who worshipped all the tarnished virtues,
went daily to his shop at eight, until
the first of three strokes forced him to retire.

He liked talking. Somebody had to listen,
so I was the listener for hours after school
until my parents called me home to supper.
We'd sit on his glassed-in porch where he kept a box
of apples wrapped in newsprint.
He told me about the time he lost a job
at the mill. Nooksack seemed to kill its young
with boredom even then, but he owned a car,
a '24 Ford. He drove it east to see

America, got as far as Spokane's desert,
sold the car and worked back on the railroad.

Sometimes he asked me what I liked to do.
I told him about the drive-in movies where
my brother, Billy, took me if I paid.
In small towns movies are the only place to go.
Not Grandfather. He said they made them better when
nobody talked, and faces told it all.
"I knew Lydia Truman Gates," he said,
"back when she was plain old Lydia Carter
down on Water Street. One time her old man
caught us spooning out to the railroad tracks.
Nearly tanned my hide. He was a fisherman—
that is, till she moved her folks to Hollywood."

I don't know why, but I simply couldn't ask
what spooning was. He seemed to talk then
more to his chair's abrasions on the floor,
more to the pale alders outside his window.
The way he said her name I couldn't ask
who was Lydia Truman Gates.

                              "Nonsense,"
was all my mother said at dinner. "His mind
went haywire in the hospital. He's old.
He makes things up and can't tell the difference."

I think my father's smile embarrassed her
when he said, "The poor guy's disappointed.
Nothing ever went right for him, so he daydreams."

"Nonsense," my mother said. "And anyway
no Lydia Truman Gates ever came
from a town like this."

                        "It's not so bad a place.
I make a pretty decent living here."

My mother huffed. While I stared past my plate
Billy asked, "Who is Lydia Truman Gates?"

It wasn't long before we all found out.
The paper ran a story on her. How
she was famous in the twenties for a while,
married the oil billionaire, Gates, and retired.
She was coming back home to Nooksack. The mayor
would give a big award and ask her help
to renovate our landmark theater.

We had better things, our mother said, to spend
our money on that some old movie house,
though she remembered how it used to look.
She said that people living in the past
wouldn't amount to much.

We didn't tell our parents where we went
that night, riding our bikes in a warm wind
past the fish houses on the Puget Sound
and up Grant Street to the Hiawatha.
Inside, Billy held my hand, and showed me
faded paintings of Indians on the walls
and dark forest patterns in the worn carpet.
The place smelled stale like old decaying clothes
shut up in a trunk for twenty years,
but Nooksack's best were there, some in tuxes,
and women stuffed into their evening gowns.
We sat on the balcony looking down
on bald heads, high hairdos and jewels.
Near the stage they had a twenty-piece band—
I still remember when the lights went out
the violins rose like a flock of birds
all at once. The drums sounded a shudder.

We saw *Morocco Gold*, *The Outlaw*, *Colonel Clay*
and the comic short, *A Bird in the Hand*,
flickering down to the screen
where Lydia Truman Gates arose in veils,
in something gossamer
astonishing even in 1965.
Lydia Truman Gates was like a dream
of lithe attention, her dark eyes laughing
at death, at poverty or a satin bed.
And when they brought her on the stage, applause
rising and falling like a tidal wave,
I had to stand up on my seat to see

a frail old woman, assisted by two men,
tiny on that distant stage.

                    My brother
yanked me past what seemed like a hundred pairs
of knees for all the times I said "Excuse us."
We ran out where the chauffeur
waiting by her limousine, his face painted
green by the light from Heilman's Piano Store,
breathing smoke. "You guys keep your distance."

"Is she coming out?"

                    He crushed his cigarette:
"No, she's gonna die in there. What do you think?"

More people joined us, pacing in the alley,
watching the chauffeur smoke by the door propped
open with a cinderblock.
And then the door half-opened, sighed back,
opened at last on the forearm of a man.

Behind him, Lydia Truman Gates stepped out
with her cane—hardly the woman I had seen
enduring all the problems of the world
with such aplomb. She stared down at the pavement,
saying, "Thank you, I can see it clearly now."

"Mrs. Gates," Billy stuttered. "Mrs. Gates."

The chauffeur tried to block us, but she said,
"That's all right, Andrew. They're just kids. I'm safe."

"Our grandpa says hello," I blurted out.

She paused for half a beat, glanced at Billy,
then peered at me as if to study terror,
smiling. "Well I'll be damned. And who's he?"

"Don't listen to him," Billy said. "He's nuts."

"George McCracken," I said, "the one you spooned with
down to the railroad tracks."

                        "George McCracken."
She straightened, looked up at the strip of sky.
"Spooned. Well, that's one way to talk about it."
She laughed from deep down in her husky lungs.
"Old Georgie McCracken. Is he still alive?
Too scared to come downtown and say hello?"
She reached out from her furs and touched my hair.
"Thanks for the message, little man. I knew him.
I knew he'd never get out of this town.
You tell your Grandpa Hi from Liddy Carter."

The man at her elbow said they had to leave.
She nodded, handing her award and purse
to the fat chauffeur.

                        Then flashbulbs started popping.
I saw her face lit up, then pale and caving

back into the darkness. "Christ," she whispered,
"get me out of here."

                 I stumbled, or was pushed.
My eyes kept seeing her exploding at me,
a woman made entirely of light
beside the smaller figure who was real.
Two men tipped her into the limousine
and it slid off like a shark, parting the crowd.

A picture ran in the next day's *Herald*—
the great actress touches a local boy.
For two weeks everybody talked about me,
but I kept thinking, *Is he still alive?*
Too scared to come downtown and say hello?

I thought of her decaying on a screen,
her ribs folding like a silk umbrella's rods,
while all the men who gathered around her
clutched at the remnants of her empty dress.

DISCLOSURE

With blue official flap and legalese
the State acknowledges an end to what
began in privacy, in passing glances.
What I remember of your voice is not
an issue lawyers willingly address,
and I've avoided their neat document.
There was a time when the word *wife* warmed me,
but as you say I think too much of words.

Many nights I raised my head from the pillow,
watched you sleeping, wife in a girl's flannel,
there by the bed your window open.
Long-stemmed, unnamable flower in whom
I was lost and saved for ten brief years,
my rancor can't contain these images:
your hair lightened to its roots by Greek sun,
my maps of married pleasure on your skin.

It's strange what we can make ourselves believe.
Memory saves, recrimination uses
every twisted syllable of the past.
Still, with all the errors I acknowledge
added to those I fail or refuse to see,
I say our marriage was a gentle thing,
a secret bargain children sometimes make
and then forget when the weather's changed.

Lawyers put it other ways. They don't know
how small exchanges still take place, of gifts
collected long ago, drawings of a house
we lived in, letters from friends we haven't told.

How separately we stumble on some object—
a book I signed, a scarf you knitted—
and call to tell the other it is there,
wondering if it will be wanted back.

BLACKENED PEACHES

One fall it was Jim and me living out
to the county. We were farmers then. A cold
northeasterly blew down like a sheet of ice,
nipped the peach trees so the leaves turned black.
All winter long the leaves was black as could be.
They never dropped, not even when it snowed,
and it scared me some to walk under the boughs,
the way they rattled so unnaturally.

We were married years when that happened. I first
come out here from Wisconsin on the train—
1902, when I was a little redhead.
I remember the train stopped in the Cascades
and I saw all the mountain sheep in the world
was crossing the tracks. You wouldn't see that now.
A man named Slaughter met the train, shouting,
"This way to the Slaughter-house!" My father said
he meant a hotel, but I was never sure.
People have been dying on me ever since.

Soon after we moved up here to Nooksack
Father passed on. I went down with a fever
and that was when Doctor Hale first come to me.
He was a tall man, not a scary one,
and you could tell he was refined. He combed
his hair back neat, wore wire glasses that looked
tiny on a man so big, always wore
a suit and carried his black leather case.
His wife I believe died five years before,

but you saw no sign of sadness in him.
Once he asked me what was my favorite fruit
and I said, "Peaches," and the next visit, why,
there was a good ripe peach waiting for me.
He called me Sally Peaches with a laugh.

On my sixteenth birthday Doctor Hale come by
in his buggy with a bucket to make ice cream.
Halfway through our party Mama left the room.
Doctor Hale and I sat in the kitchen,
him with his hands on his knees, looking shy.
After a while he took his glasses off,
rubbed them with his handkerchief. His eyes was tired.
"Sally Peaches," he said. "You're too big for that.
I promise I won't baby you again."

He brought a box in from his buggy for me:
"I think, Sally, you're old enough for this."
The most beautiful party dress I ever saw
lay inside with its lace sleeves open to me.
Doctor Hale said he'd been saving it for years.
"I can tell it's going to fit you perfectly."

The next time I was over to town I walked
right by his office. I heard an axe's sound
from his yard, tiptoed up to have a look.
There was Doctor Hale stripped to the waist
except for his specs and braces, swinging
that axe as if he were a younger man.
When he paused to wipe his brow I could see
he looked angry, tired, or not right with himself.

He seemed to want to tear those logs apart
with bare hands. I left before he saw me,
but that night I kept seeing him, the way
all gentleness went out of him when he swung.

One day, though nobody was sick, he come
again to our house. Mother left us alone
and Doctor Hale stood awkwardly and looked
down at me through his lenses. We were quiet
so you could hear the rain clap on the roof.
I give him a flower from the kitchen vase;
he fingered it like something that was ill.
"Sally," he said, "tell me what I look like."

He smiled strangely and I suppose I blushed
and couldn't raise my eyes to look at him.
"No," he said. "I know how I look. I look old.
Old enough to have been worn out working when
your father was sick. I never told you that
because I held some rather strange ideas.
You know, of course, I'm very fond of you."
He coughed at the flower in his spotted hands.
"But I developed these peculiar ideas.
What I mean is that now you're growing up.
You've had a lonely childhood in some ways,
but you're a woman and you'll marry soon
and then with luck you'll never be alone.
I'm wishing you good luck. Good health. All good."
Each word he spoke then seemed to weaken him,
and when he drove away I sat there crying
though I couldn't tell my mother what it meant.

I was only seventeen when I met Jim.
He lumberjacked in the camp out to the lake.
I always liked the woods, so green and nice,
the ferns in bunches, trees covered in moss.
When I was little I was scared to walk
alone for fear the Indians would get me,
but Jim made the woods seem lighter than before.
His family was Welsh. They all was singers.
Next to Doctor Hale you'd think he was small,
more my size, but he was a strong camp boss.
Men always said he was good to work for.
Once he let his whiskers grow like the men
and I said they was awful-looking things.
"What's the matter, Sally," says he. "Seen a ghost?"

"Jim," I says, "you've ruined your face."

                        "Ruined?"

I told him I wouldn't stand for any man
who looked like a porcupine. That day he shaved.
He had wavy black hair and shiny eyes,
could eat like a mule and still dance all night.
He used to say there was music in the Welsh
and fight in the Norse—that's the stock I come from.
Jim was always a truthful husband, and I
told him only the one white lie. I said
my father used to call me Sally Peaches.

I suppose I wanted Jim to call me that,
but it never felt right when he said the name.

Then one year that northeasterly come down.
We'd been on the farm a while. Jim bought the place
so I wouldn't have to cook in a camp.
There was peach trees on it just for me, he said.
The cold he caught in that storm turned bad,
sank down in his lungs and worked there rasping him
with pain. I sent a neighbor for Doctor Hale
and all day set with a fear he wouldn't come.
Finally I heard his buggy—he never
his whole life would drive a car—stop outside,
and saw him stoop to come in at the door.
He went to work while I stayed in the kitchen
brewing tea. Outside the leaves was blackened,
rattling in the wind like sick men breathing.
Made me dizzy just to think of it.

When Doctor Hale come out he was pasty and old.
He took his glasses off, rubbed a sore spot
on the bridge of his nose, give me a flat look.
He said, "Jim's been asking for Sally Peaches."
There we were in the kitchen, six feet apart
and silent as the frost on the windowpanes.

The black leaves was death, though. I knew for sure
they would take someone. That year Mama died.
That year, while the trees was still all blighted,
Doctor Hale was killed. His horse took a fright
out on Mountainview Road, pulled his buggy

off a bridge and threw him into the river.
There's foxes on the road. People suppose
it was the foxes give that horse such a scare.

You never saw so big a funeral
as his. The church spilled people into the street.
The paper said a whole era was gone.
He was the last of the horse and buggy doctors.

You won't believe me, but I saw him again.
I tell you I saw him here in this very room
twenty-two years ago, the year Jim died.
It wasn't too long after Kennedy
that Jim took sick again and I could see
the blood draining out of his face, his lips
a pale purple, skin damp and hands ice cold.
I did the only thing I knew to do
and prayed to God not to take him away.

It was dark. The house rattled in a wind.
I sat there in the kitchen by the stove
muttering this prayer, and the room changed.
I wasn't alone any more.
I turned and saw a man beside the door,
knew him by the wire rims of his glasses,
his smile peaceful though he was made of rain.
I heard his voice with so much gentleness:
"Sally, hush, all our illnesses will end."
When he said my name it was like the sound

grew inside me till the tears just had to fall.
I could almost feel his big hand on my hair.
By the time I dried my eyes he was gone.

For eight long months Jim wasted away.
I remember cursing God for what he did
and I know in his heart how Jim cursed God.
Sometimes I wanted Doctor Hale to come,
but the dead can't be faithful anymore.
I got up in the middle of every night
to give Jim his pills. Already it was like
I lived alone in a house with many voices.

One of those nights I saw he'd gone at last.
I didn't know what to do. I didn't know
why I thought there was one more thing to do,
a last thing, because Jim was Welsh and I knew
there was something you had to do for the Welsh.

I thought about how fine he used to look.
How his eyes was bright. How he sang at camp.
I looked out the window and could feel him
lying there in the cold bed at my back.
I knew what he was telling me, and left
the window open for his soul to go.

BIOGRAPHICAL NOTE

David Mason is the former Poet Laureate of Colorado. His previous books of poems include *Sea Salt: Poems of a Decade*, *The Country I Remember*, and *Arrivals*. His verse novel, *Ludlow*, won the Colorado Book Award and was featured on the *PBS News-Hour*. Mason is the author of three essay collections, including *Voices, Places* and a memoir, *News from the Village*. He wrote the libretti for Lori Laitman's opera of *The Scarlet Letter* and for Tom Cipullo's award-winning *After Life*. Mason divides his time between Colorado and Tasmania, and teaches at Colorado College.

CPSIA information can be obtained
at www.ICGtesting.com
Printed in the USA
BVOW09s1602060318
509774BV00003B/3/P